tchaikovsky

compact companions

PHILIPS *Classics*

COMPACT COMPANIONS

TCHAIKOVSKY

DAVID NICE

SIMON & SCHUSTER

NEW YORK LONDON TORONTO SYDNEY TOKYO SINGAPORE

SIMON & SCHUSTER
ROCKEFELLER CENTER
1230 AVENUE OF THE AMERICAS
NEW YORK, NEW YORK 10020

Designed by Wherefore Art? Edited by Emma Lawson.

Printed and bound in Singapore by Imago Publishing Ltd.
10 9 8 7 6 5 4 3 2 1

Library of Congress Cataloging-in-Publication data
Nice, David, 1962–
Tchaikovsky/David Nice.
p. cm. — (Compact companions)
Discography: p.
Includes bibliographical references (p.).
ISBN 0-684-81357-2
1. Tchaikovsky, Peter Ilich, 1840–1893. 2. Composers—Russia—Biography. I. Series.
ML410. C4N53 1995
780.′ 92—dc20
[B]   95-3359
CIP
MN

Front cover picture reproduced by kind permission of Bradford Art Galleries and Museums,
Bridgeman Art Library

CONTENTS

*Pyotr Ilyich
Tchaikovsky
1840-1893
(Mansell)*

On January 1, 1893, the year of his death, Tchaikovsky paid a visit to his old nanny Fanny Dürbach, then living in the small town of Montbéliard in France. His childhood came alive with astonishing vividness: 'After a gap of forty-four years to see someone once held in close affection, to recall the past as though it had happened only yesterday – it's a unique experience,' he wrote to his brother Anatoly.

The French governess had joined the Tchaikovsky household in the town of Votkinsk, 600 miles east of Moscow, in 1844, when Pyotr Ilyich was four and a half. Yet although she may have been more demonstrative in her endearments than Tchaikovsky's mother, Alexandra Andreyevna Tchaikovskaya, she never took pride of place in his affections, and it was above all her revelation of 'some extremely nice letters from mother' which left the fifty-two-year-old composer so deeply moved. Never anything but truthful in his correspondence, Tchaikovsky paid a tribute in simple words to his patroness and confidante Nadezhda von Meck: 'My mother was a marvellous, intelligent woman who was passionately fond of her children,' though he was honest enough to add at a later stage that he had loved her 'with a sort of morbidly passionate love'.

The infinite kindness of Ilya Petrovich Tchaikovsky, the composer's 'saintly papa', seems to have been taken rather more for granted. A diligent mining engineer who was manager of the Votkinsk iron works, his musical education had been brief and his interest in opera and theater remained limited, but he did respond with tears of emotion to the weekly performances he attended, and he was to prove a model of

Tchaikovsky's parents, Alexandra Andreyevna ...
(AKG)

supportiveness when his second son finally settled on a composing career. He was already a widower with a four-year-old daughter, Zinaida, when he married Alexandra Assier, eighteen years his junior, in 1833. Their first surviving child was Nikolay, born in 1838; Pyotr Ilyich followed on May 7, 1840, and by the time Fanny Dürbach arrived as governess there was also a daughter, Alexandra (Sasha) and a third son, Ippolit. On the evidence of a letter from Ilya to his wife, Sasha shared the credit (though it seems unlikely for a two-year-old) of Tchaikovsky's first composition, the song 'Our mama in St. Petersburg', written while Alexandra was away on her nanny-hunt in 1844.

Tchaikovsky was born at a time when the Russian arts as we know them today were still in their infancy. Pushkin, the 'father of Russian literature', had died three years earlier, killed in the same kind of senseless duel he had described so vividly in his masterly novel in verse, *Eugene Onegin*. His works would have played a part in the young

Tchaikovsky's education, though when Fanny Dürbach dubbed her protégé 'le petit Pouchkine', she was thinking of his proficiency in French, rather than Russian, verse (and it was Joan of Arc, not Catherine the Great, who dominated his seven-year-old imagination). As for music, the founder of a specifically Russian school of composition, Mikhail Glinka, was still alive. Like an earlier generation of Russian composers, he had fallen under the spell of the Italian opera which held sway in St. Petersburg; paradoxically, it took three years in Italy to kindle a love of mother Russia which gained the upper hand in the first great nationalist opera, *A Life for the Tsar*, in 1836. An entry in the mature Tchaikovsky's diary sums up his thoughts on the matter:

... and Ilya Petrovich (circa 1860) (Lebrecht)

Glinka. *An unprecedented astounding phenomenon in the world of art. A dilettante ... who wrote nothing apart from banalities in the taste of the thirties; and who then suddenly, at the age of thirty-four, produced an opera which, in its inspiration, its scope, its novelty, its immaculate technique, stands alongside all that is greatest and most profound in art.*

Glinka went on to greater heights of musical sophistication in his second opera *Ruslan and Ludmila*, based, like so many works to come, on a Pushkin fantasy. But it was *A Life for the Tsar* which Tchaikovsky held in greater reverence, simply because that was the Glinka opera he saw first, as a ten-year-old in St. Petersburg. As he pointed out later in his capacity as a music critic, 'The aesthetic ecstasies which one experiences in one's early years are of enormous significance and leave a trace which lasts throughout one's life.' A greater ecstasy even than his first hearing of *A Life for the Tsar* was his discovery of Mozart's *Don Giovanni* several years later:

The music of Don Giovanni *was the first music to have a really shattering effect on me. It took me through into that world of artistic beauty where only the greatest geniuses dwell. It is to Mozart that I am indebted for the fact that I have dedicated my life to music. He was the first to stir my musical powers and it was he who caused me to love music more than anything in the world.*

Tchaikovsky had his not very musical family to thank for steering him towards the purer air of Mozart; as he pointed out to von Meck, his parents' lack of interest in contemporary music saved him, at least in the crucial years of development, from the 'Byronic spirit of despair and disillusionment' which marked his own, romantic century. As one of that century's most impassioned spokesmen, he would come to value the counterbalance of Mozart all the more: 'Perhaps it is precisely because as a

Letter in French from the eight-year-old Tchaikovsky to his nurse, Fanny Dürbach (Lebrecht) man of my times I am broken and morally sick that I so love to seek peace and consolation in Mozart's music,' he wrote shortly after the greatest crisis in his life. Equilibrium restored, he went on to pay homage to Mozart in the piquant arrangements of his Fourth Suite ('Mozartiana') Op.61, and the pastoral interlude which breaks the gloom (or the tension, if you find the quarter-hour divertissement superfluous) of *The Queen of Spades*, Op.68.

His first acquaintance with Mozart's opera *Don Giovanni* came from the mechanical renditions of Zerlina's 'Batti, batti' and 'Vedrai carino' on an orchestrion, a kind of portable organ which also played extracts from Bellini, Donizetti and Rossini (the Italian opera he was to see for himself, and heartily approve, during his student days in St. Petersburg). But, viewed in retrospect, that was still only 'semi-music' compared to Mozart.

Last, but by no means least for Tchaikovsky's development as a composer, was the vein of folk music which burns brightest in his early works but is never far away in any of his masterpieces. Again he explains to von Meck:

> *This occurs because I grew up in the wilds and was steeped from my earliest childhood in the indescribable beauty of Russian folk music with all its special characteristics, because I am passionately fond of the Russian element in all its manifestations, because, to put it briefly, I am a* Russian *in the fullest sense of the word.*

And so he was, to a far greater degree than those who conveniently label him a 'Western' composer simply to distinguish him from the Russian national school of composers. As we shall see, there is no such easy division to be made.

Red Square, Moscow, in the mid-nineteenth century (AKG)

The Votkinsk years, though they laid the seed for so many of Tchaikovsky's passions and characteristics in later life, came to an abrupt end when he was ten years old. He gained his first whirlwind impressions of Moscow when Ilya left Votkinsk with the family to take up a new post there, and of St. Petersburg when Ilya's trusting nature lost him the Moscow job to a colleague who abused his confidence to secure the position for himself. While their father was anxiously trying to negotiate employment elsewhere on his Petersburg rounds, Pyotr and Nikolai attended the well-to-do Schmelling boarding school as day pupils. It was an unsettling experience: they arrived in the middle of the term, and the boy missed his old nurse – Fanny had reluctantly left the family's service – and life in Votkinsk. He took music lessons from the pianist Filippov, making great advances on the Votkinsk studies he had begun under the tutelage of a liberated serf, Mariya Palchikova; but the stress of his new environment meant that, unlike his brother, he made no quick recovery from a bout of measles and was advised by doctors to suspend all activities indefinitely. By the time he was well again, the family had moved once more. Ilya's new post this time took him to Alapayevsk, which is even further east than Votkinsk, in the Ural mountains between Russia and Siberia. Pyotr improved his pianistic skills as family accompanist, but for all the new ease of his surroundings, he was now (wrote Alexandra to Fanny Dürbach) impatient, tearful and sullen. So began his adolescence.

In the summer of 1850, Tchaikovsky was enrolled in the preparatory class of St. Petersburg's School of Jurisprudence: so at the tender age of ten a future career as a lawyer was decided (family plans were originally to have him following in his father's footsteps as a mining engineer). Even so, the ever-thoughtful Ilya wrote to his wife from Alapayevsk that she should look to her son's musical education, too, since 'it would be a pity to abandon a cause half-way through'.

The parting from his mother was 'one of the most terrible days' of Tchaikovsky's life, and his letters to his family over the next two years show how he idealized his 'angelic, saintly' parents. The blow of separation was second only to the death of Alexandra Tchaikovskaya on June 13, 1854, from an outbreak of cholera which very nearly carried away Ilya too. No record survives of the boy's reactions, but in 1877 he revealed how strong his grief remained, writing to Nadezhda von Meck of his thoughts on life after death:

> *Though I deny eternal life, I still indignantly reject the notion that I will never, never see again some of my dear ones. Despite the telling force of my convictions, I can never reconcile myself again to the thought that my mother, whom I loved so much and who was such a fine person, has vanished for ever and that I will never have the opportunity of saying to her that after twenty-three years of being parted I love her just as much.*

Four years before her sudden death, Alexandra had given birth to twins, Anatoly and Modest. Pyotr was especially fond of them and, he later wrote, 'From the first moment that they were orphans, I *wanted* to be to them what a mother is to her children because I know from my own experience how a mother's tenderness and a mother's endearments have a lasting influence on a child's nature.' The consequent bond of 'mutual affection which is rare even amongst brothers' lasted until Tchaikovsky's death, and it was in his letters to the twins, especially Modest, that he was to share the secrets denied even to his soulmate Nadezhda von Meck.

Tchaikovsky's ten years as a law student passed otherwise without event. He was an average pupil; mediocre in the kindest sense of the word, he came thirteenth in his class before graduating in 1859. His musical activities still gave no signs of genius, present or future, as his piano teacher from 1855 to 1858, Rudolf Kündinger, later had the humility to recollect (only the pupil's free improvisations, he said, had been anything vaguely out of the ordinary). The only really musical member of the family, Tchaikovsky's aunt Ekaterina, taught him to take the part of Rossini's princess Semiramide in one of those virtuoso duets which require dazzling technique – he trilled rather well, apparently – and the singing teacher on the staff of the School of Jurisprudence, Gavriil Lomakin, encouraged his skill as a treble in church liturgies. His concern for the tradition of Russian Orthodox music was to remain strong throughout his life, and the raptures he felt for Italian opera (later modified) were encouraged by his friendship with another singing teacher, the single-minded Neapolitan Luigi Piccioli, whom he met in 1856.

Tchaikovsky was a popular student who made friends easily. He was regarded as literary enough for the company of his contemporary Alexey Apukhtin, who later fulfilled his promise as a leading Russian poet (Tchaikovsky was to set several of his verses as songs), and his closest friend, Vladimir Adamov, made a brilliant career as a lawyer. According to Alexandra Orlova, who as archivist of the Tchaikovsky Museum at Klin, has had unique access to documentation on the composer's life, he also came to love 'whole-heartedly and unrequitedly' his fellow student Vladimir Gerard, the first indication we have of his homosexual nature. If the well-authenticated version of Tchaikovsky's death is true – a suicide forced on him by a 'court of law' made up of former students from the School of Jurisprudence – then

The reluctant civil servant:
Tchaikovsky in 1861 (AKG)

the dutiful speech Gerard made at his grave is doubly ironic.

If his schooldays were unremarkable, then Tchaikovsky's short-lived career as a clerk in the Ministry of Justice – from June 1859 until September 1863 – confirmed that he would never go far in the legal profession. Ilya continued to offer the support his son so badly needed to believe in his future as a composer. 'Father insists that it is still not too late for me to take it up professionally. I would like to think that he is right but the trouble is that if I have any ability it's quite impossible to make anything of it now. They've made a civil servant out of me – and a bad one at that,' he wrote to his sister Sasha in March 1861, four months after her wedding to Lev Davydov. At this time, the Davydovs would have been much preoccupied with the changes wrought on the family estate at Kamenka by Alexander II's decree emancipating the Russian serfs – a liberal move which would no doubt have been welcomed by Sasha's husband. His father had been involved in the ill-fated Decembrist uprising of 1825 against the repressive regime of Nicholas I, and his mother – who outlived Tchaikovsky by two years, dying in 1895 at the age of ninety-three – fascinated the future composer of *Eugene Onegin* with memories of Pushkin (a Decembrist sympathizer) as well as of her hard life in Siberian exile with her husband following the disastrous end of the revolt. The estate at Kamenka came to play an important role in providing Tchaikovsky with the security and the family atmosphere he found increasingly vital.

For the moment, he used his modest salary to lead the conventionally elegant life of a fancy-free St. Petersburger, plunging into the social round of operas, plays and parties, going through the motions of flirtatious encounters with young women who found him attractive. It seems unlikely that he took any steps to realize his true sexuality; the one solitary mention of the matter seems to suggest that he actually backed away from it. His first chance to travel abroad was as interpreter and secretary to Vasily Pisarev, a friend of his father's, and although he had vivid impressions of 'dowdy' Berlin and amusing Hamburg, bathed industriously at Ostend and relished 'several thousand voices' belting Handel's Hallelujah Chorus in London (which he found 'gloomy' in the rain), his relationship with Pisarev deteriorated towards the end of the journey and cast a pall over the whole experience. 'You remember Pisarev?' he wrote to Sasha. 'Imagine that beneath that mask of *bonhomie* from which I took him to be an unpolished but worthy gentleman, there are hidden the most vile qualities of mind. Up till then I had not suspected that such incredibly base persons existed on this earth.' Such hinting at vague horrors gives rise to the reasonable supposition that Pisarev may have made sexual advances to his 'secretary', and that Tchaikovsky, hardly yet come to terms with his own nature, reacted with a disproportionate sense of revulsion.

In any case, he wrote in the same letter, disaffection with his own financial extravagance and 'unhappiness in *love*' had made him turn his thoughts to acquiring a technique of musical composition: 'I have been studying thorough-bass, and it's going extremely well. Who knows, perhaps in three years you'll be hearing my operas and singing my arias.' He had taken up the studies he mentions with Nikolay Zaremba, once a lawyer like Tchaikovsky and now the Russian Musical Society's teacher of musical theory. It says a great deal about the slow laying of foundations for a national school of music that the RMS had been founded as recently as 1859, the first of its kind. The driving force behind it was the pianist and composer Anton Rubinstein, who wielded his reputation to win the tsar's approval and a good home for the Society in the residence of the grand duchess, the Mikhailovsky Palace (a splendid if rather overwhelming edifice built between 1797 and 1800 for mad, pug-nosed Tsar Paul I, who was murdered there in 1801, it is now known as the Engineers' Castle). Zaremba's reputation has suffered as a result of the fierce opposition fielded by the 'free' school of Russian composers with Balakirev at their head, but there is no doubt that this rather dry, disciplinarian figure, whose sympathies stopped short at Mendelssohn, helped Tchaikovsky take the first steps in the study of strict counterpoint he so badly needed.

Less than a year later, in September 1862, Tchaikovsky was one of the first pupils at the newly opened St. Petersburg Conservatoire, a natural consequence of the RMS's success story. Zaremba continued to lead Tchaikovsky forward in the art of composition; the young composer also took classes in flute and piano. But he was still working at the Ministry, even if, in that true Russian bureaucratic style so brilliantly lampooned by the writer Gogol, he spent most of the time twiddling his thumbs; and as he wrote to his sister, 'I shall not finally give up work until I am finally sure that I am an artist and not a civil servant.'

That step came the following September, and it cannot have been easy. Tchaikovsky's father, with whom he had been living in harmony for some time, had long been leading a precarious financial existence. In 1857 he had entrusted his life savings to a swindler, and lost it, while in the spring of 1863 he resigned his post as Director of the St. Petersburg Institute of Technology after clashes with the authorities, retiring on a modest pension (yet there was happiness in store: in 1865 he was to marry his housekeeper of the past two years, Elizaveta Alexandrova, whose generosity of spirit Tchaikovsky soon came to cherish). Under the circumstances,

Rimsky-Korsakow

83

The 'Mighty Handful': Rimsky-Korsakov (1895) (AKG)

Ilya's continued encouragement amazed his son all the more. He later recounted it with emotion to Nadezhda von Meck:

Although it pained my father that I had not fulfilled his hopes of an administrative career, although it could not but grieve him to see that I was willing to endure poverty to become a musician, he never so much as by a single word made me feel that he was displeased. He simply took a keen and enthusiastic interest in my plans and intentions and gave me every encouragement. I owe him so very, very much. I do not know what would have become of me if fate had given me a wilful tyrant for a father.

His stern older brother Nikolai, however, disapproved, and Sasha was apprehensive. Tchaikovsky eloquently pleaded his case with her, pointing out that he had abandoned the dandyish extravagances which had been his only consolation as a clerk at the Ministry and adding that he was 'certain only of one thing: that I shall become a good musician, and that I'll never be without my daily bread'. He stayed with his father, scraping a living by giving piano lessons and tuition in the musical theory he had learned from Zaremba.

Tchaikovsky never had cause to regret his diligent studies at the St. Petersburg Conservatoire, while his most outstanding contemporary would look back on the *laissez-faire* philosophy of the alternative circle which gathered around Balakirev with some ruefulness. In his remarkably candid autobiography, Nikolai Rimsky-Korsakov writes of his own musical education at the time that Tchaikovsky entered the Conservatoire:

The 'Mighty Handful': Balakirev (1870) (AKG)

What did I need? A piano technique, the technique of harmony and counterpoint, and an idea of musical forms. Balakirev should have made me sit down at the piano and learn to play well. That was so easy for him, as I worshipped him and obeyed his advice in everything. But he did not do it; declaring from the outset that I was no pianist, he gave up the whole thing as altogether unnecessary. He should have given me a few lessons in harmony and counterpoint, should have made me write a few fugues and explained the grammar of musical forms to me. He could not do it, as he had not studied systematically himself and considered it unnecessary ...

As the founding father of this free school of composers formed in opposition to what he saw as the rigors of the St. Petersburg Conservatoire, Balakirev had forceful ideas and natural talent, but not the technical knowledge to pass on to the four other gifted composers in his circle. Yet, since Mussorgsky was a retired imperial guard, Borodin a full-time professor of chemistry, César Cui an engineering officer and the teenage Rimsky-Korsakov a naval cadet, none of them boasting a formal education, technical knowledge was exactly what they needed.

Unfortunately, an artificial distinction was soon made – and has persisted – between this circle known as the 'Five' and the Conservatoire-trained composers. The 'mighty handful', as they came to be called, were supposed to be iconoclastic, unfettered and profoundly Russian, while their opposite numbers, including Tchaikovsky and later the brilliantly precocious Glazunov, remained hopelessly Westernized and deeply conservative. Tchaikovsky came to resent this labeling, especially because it fueled false rumors that he and Rimsky-Korsakov hated each other. In 1892 he summed up with his usual clarity and fair-mindedness:

The 'Mighty Handful':
Cesar Cui, portrait by
Repin (1890) (AKG)

According to the accepted view of the Russian musical public, I belong to that party which is hostile to the Russian composer whom I love and admire more than any other alive: Rimsky-Korsakov. He is the finest ornament of the 'New Russian School'; but I belong to the old, retrograde school. Why? Rimsky-Korsakov has been subject to the influences of his time to a greater or lesser extent, and so have I ... In short, despite all the differences of our musical natures we are, it would seem, travelling along the same road; and, for my part, I am proud to have such a companion on the journey. And yet I am supposed to belong to the party which is opposed to Rimsky-Korsakov. There is a strange misunderstanding here which has had, and still has, regrettable consequences ... it accentuates the extremes at both ends and ultimately it compromises us, the musicians, in the eyes of future generations.

By this time, Rimsky-Korsakov had himself acquired a Conservatoire education: as professor, he also became the establishment's most diligent pupil and only with this thorough schooling behind him did he go on to write his three orchestral masterpieces – *Scheherazade*, the *Russian Easter Festival* Overture and *Capriccio espagnol* – in the single season of 1877–8. And as we shall see, Tchaikovsky was to have more dealings with Balakirev, and consequently to develop a bolder strain of nationalism than he is sometimes given credit for.

At the end of Tchaikovsky's first full season at the Conservatoire – surviving evidence of which remains only a few undistinguished exercises to add to the equally unremarkable songs of his pre-Conservatoire days – his principal teacher of composition and head of the Conservatoire, Anton Rubinstein, set him the task of writing a large-scale orchestral piece. He took as his subject high drama, *The Storm*, by the playwright Russians still regard as the founding father of their theatrical tradition, Alexandr Ostrovsky. Recent revival of British interest in his plays has centered around his Gogolian-style comedy *Too Clever By Half*, in a madcap production by Richard Jones; his tragic vein has entered immortality via opera and Janácek's setting of *The Storm*, *Katya Kabanova* (1921). Tchaikovsky took up the atmosphere and the key dramatic moments of the tale, in which a guilty wife confesses her adultery at the height of a ferocious storm and is driven to suicide – drowning in the Volga – by the persecution of her mother-in-law. In his Introduction, he broke the cardinal rules of the sober-scoring Rubinstein by including harp and cor anglais (soon to become a trademark of poignant love in his scores); but the presentation is rather more interesting than the thematic substance. In that respect his next symphonic poem, *Fatum*, Op.77, was to show more characteristic traits, and in his first true masterpiece, *Romeo and Juliet*, he would eventually solve the problem of how to develop the action. Here, the heightening of Katya's guilt, as counterpointed with the storm, moves forward stiffly in an academic fugato passage (like a fugue, where different orchestral voices enter in imitation of each other), and the love music has nowhere to go. Tchaikovsky employed it again, differently scored and paced, as nothing more than a preface to the main theme of his inspired slow movement in the First Symphony, and *The Storm*, Op.76, was never published in his lifetime. Even so, it remains a distinguished orchestral starting point.

Because of Anton Rubinstein's disapproval, relayed to Tchaikovsky by his friend and fellow student (later critic) Herman Laroche, who bore the brunt of the conservative master's fury when he delivered his colleague's piece, *The Storm*, was not the first of Tchaikovsky's compositions to be performed. That honor went to the *Characteristic Dances*, soon to be incorporated into his opera *The Voyevoda*, Op.3. The première took place during the summer of 1865 in the beautiful gardens of the tsarist palace of Pavlovsk, and the conductor of the evening's light entertainment was none other than Johann Strauss, the waltz king. Oddly, Tchaikovsky knew nothing of the occasion and arrived in St. Petersburg to discover that this auspicious first performance had taken place the previous day. He had been working, back at his sister's and brother-in-law's Kamenka estate, on an Overture in C minor. It was followed dutifully by another, this time in F, during the following term at the Conservatoire, and by a single movement for string quartet which includes a folksong noted down at Kamenka. That folksong was to reappear in the first of two piano pieces which make up Tchaikovsky's official Opus 1, and the rich native soil of his favorite family home would yield an even more distinguished folk melody to be worked into the slow movement of his String Quartet No. 1, Op.11 – the *Andante cantabile*, which, in various arrangements, was to become one of Tchaikovsky's best-loved themes.

Tchaikovsky made his conducting debut with the F major Overture nervously, but with nothing like the near-disastrous results which nearly brought an 1868 performance of the *Characteristic Dances* in their new *Voyevoda* dress to a halt (the process of overcoming podium-fright was to be an agonizing one when he attempted it again in later life, but once mastered, his ability to present his own works around the world was to give him tremendous satisfaction).

His final task before graduating in December 1865 was to write a cantata on Schiller's 'Ode to Joy', with the Finale of Beethoven's Ninth Symphony as a

The brothers
Rubinstein: Anton by
Repin (AKG) …

daunting example presumably not to be imitated. Tchaikovsky's cantata is a sober, Conservatoire-oriented occasional piece, worthy neither of Laroche's well-meaning hyperbole when he praised it as the greatest musical event in Russia since *Judith* by the then well-regarded composer Serov, nor of Anton Rubinstein's opprobrium and a blast from the Balakirev circle in the shape of a negative article by César Cui. This did not appear in print until the following April, and its effect upon Tchaikovsky serves as a warning to all critics in handling the young and sensitive. 'When I read that frightful judgment, I don't know what I did with myself,' Tchaikovsky wrote. 'All day I wandered aimlessly through the city, repeating "I'm sterile, insignificant, nothing will come out of me, I'm ungifted ..." Tchaikovsky's own opinion of the cantata can hardly have been favorable, for to Rubinstein's further annoyance, he absented himself from the first performance and the medal-giving ceremony.

None of this prevented Rubinstein's brother, Nikolay, from appointing Tchaikovsky teacher of musical theory at the St. Petersburg Royal Musical Society's opposite-number establishment in Moscow, a post which he left to take up immediately after his graduation in January 1866. 'I am living at [Nikolay] Rubinstein's,' he wrote to Anatoly and Modest shortly after his arrival in Moscow:

He is a very kind and agreeable man, quite lacking that element of unapproachability which one finds in his brother. I occupy a small room next to his bedroom and when we go to bed at night (which, I might say, looks like being a very rare occurrence) I am, to tell the truth, somewhat embarrassed because I am frightened that even the squeak of my pen will stop him getting to sleep (there is only a thin partition between us) and I really am terribly busy.

... and Nikolay
(Mansell)

Rubinstein seems to have mothered Tchaikovsky during his first months in Moscow, buying him clothes to supplement his meager income from his new Conservatoire post and adding the finishing touch in the shape of a frock coat left behind by the famous Polish violinist Wieniawski, then teaching at the St. Petersburg Conservatoire. Tchaikovsky also made loyal friends who were to stand by him – Nikolay Kashkin, future Conservatoire professor and music critic, the administrator and cellist Konstantin Albrecht, and the enterprising music publisher Pyotr Jurgenson – and took on several private pupils, including the fourteen-year-old Vladimir Shilovsky, whose brother Konstantin was to work with him on the scenario for *Eugene Onegin*, Op. 24.

Flirtations with female pupils, as well as the old, familiar round of theater-going and the intoxicating success of his F major Overture as conducted by Nikolai Rubinstein made him feel still more at home in Moscow. What shattered his nerves were Cui's notice on the cantata and his burning the candle at both ends, working throughout the summer on his First Symphony, Op.13. His worries that the symphony 'just would not come' were later confirmed by Modest, who claimed that it gave him the most trouble of all his symphonies. This project, which must have meant so much to Tchaikovsky at a crucial stage in his career, was interrupted by the composition of another overture – his best yet – this time to celebrate the Moscow visit of the Tsarevich and his Danish bride (hence the effective marrying together of the Danish and Russian anthems in his Festival Overture, Op.15, a feat of which Tchaikovsky remained infinitely more proud than he ever was of the later, much more famous *1812* Overture). Despite the now-familiar negative response from Anton Rubinstein in St. Petersburg, Tchaikovsky continued to work on and revise his First Symphony, which he gave the vaguely programatic title of *Winter Daydreams* and gave evocative names to the first two movements accordingly. Yet although the more sympathetic Nikolay conducted individual movements throughout the winter of 1866–7, it was not until 1868 that he was ready to give the première of the complete symphony, and even though that was a success, it was not immediately taken into the repertoire.

It is hard to understand why, especially since Russia was at that time hardly rich in symphonies to call her own. Anton Rubinstein's contributions to the genre showed a sober dependence on the German tradition, and Cui was ostentatiously snubbing them when, in 1865, he welcomed the new E♭ minor symphony of the seventeen-year-old Rimsky-Korsakov as the first true Russian specimen of its kind. Yet even in its 1884 revision for student and amateur orchestras, Rimsky's modest contribution hardly counts. And since Balakirev took some thirty-five years to complete what should have been the true pioneering example, that leaves the first symphonies of Tchaikovsky and Borodin to lead the field. Tchaikovsky would not have been familiar with Borodin's work in 1866 – it was not performed until three years later – and yet there is plenty of common ground. Although Balakirev's circle favored the progressive examples of Berlioz and Liszt, Schumann was the ideal for all Russian composers in the 1860s, and there are moments in both symphonies where Borodin and Tchaikovsky respectively pay tribute. However, where Borodin's admiration is mixed with homage to Beethoven, Tchaikovsky's is supported by delicate imitation of Mendelssohn (it is not surprising to learn that he was playing through Mendelssohn's 'Italian' Symphony as well as Schumann's First and Third in piano arrangements in between bouts of composition).

More important in both cases is the rhythmic ingenuity – Borodin is slightly the more daring here, but Tchaikovsky makes good use of dramatic accents in his Scherzo (adapted from a piano sonata of the previous year). Above all, a true Russian voice sounds from time to time. The cut and the solo-clarinet coloring of the wistful second theme in Tchaikovsky's first movement ('Reveries of a Winter Journey') sound distinctly like Borodin in Polovtsian mode. Yet in his Adagio cantabile Tchaikovsky created the first great melody he could truly call his own. It is not based on a Russian folksong, nor does it begin like one, and yet within its long span there are unmistakable elements and contours of 'mother Russia', the kind of authentic Russian spirit we hear at the start of Mussorgsky's *Boris Godunov*. Tchaikovsky is especially skillful in building his entire movement – with the exception of the *Storm* love music reworked for the picture-frame – on parts of this melody. He was not, at this stage, very happy with the conventions of sonata form as laid out in the symphonies of the Austro-German tradition – the need to present your themes, to develop them rigorosly and then to provide a satisfying recapitulation – but when the tune leads the way, as in this slow movement, he proved himself second to none. It is hardly surprising that at the first performance, as he informed Anatoly, 'The Adagio was a great success.' But the symphony as a whole contains much attractive music – even the sometimes stiff and formal Finale makes the most of what is, this time, a genuine Russian folksong – and Tchaikovsky should have the last word on it, writing to Nadezhda von Meck in 1883: 'Although it is in many ways very immature, yet fundamentally it has more substance and is better than many of my other more mature works.'

He was not consciously cultivating a nationalist vein in the symphony. Yet he

The 'Mighty Handful': Borodin (Lebrecht)

could hardly avoid it in his next work, which he began in November 1866, two months after the opening of the new Moscow Conservatoire – which he celebrated in true Russian style by playing Glinka's Overture to *Ruslan and Ludmila* on the piano, from memory. His own thoughts had turned to opera, especially since the Moscow circles in which he moved had won him a firm friend and card-playing companion in Ostrovsky, and he must have been flattered when the playwright offered to make a libretto for him out of his colorful drama *The Voyevoda* (*The Provincial Governor*). Tchaikovsky repaid Ostrovsky's graciousness poorly by losing the first-act libretto and suggesting to this master craftsman how the dramatic scheme might best be reorganized. The gradual retreat of Ostrovsky, and Tchaikovsky's subsequent role in shaping the rest of the scenario left an operatic melodrama that was to no one's satisfaction. His brother Modest voiced the chief criticism:

Everything that comprises the main charm and enchantment of the comedy – that is, all the real-life and fantastic part of it – was ruthlessly omitted, and only the pallid and empty story of the unsuccessful amorous adventure of a lascivious and cruel old man {the eponymous Provincial Governor} was preserved. There is no trace in the opera of the lively and colourful folk scenes, nor of the detailed delineation, so vivid and striking, of less important characters.

In other words, this was not the world of *Boris Godunov*, which Mussorgsky was still working on and which would in due time take its place as the true operatic successor of Glinka's two masterpieces. Even so, the première of *The Voyevoda*, which took place at Moscow's Bolshoi Theatre in February 1869 after endless vagaries, was a modest success, though that did not prevent Tchaikovsky from destroying the score years later.

Latter-day resurrection from surviving orchestral parts reveals flashes of inspiration and some skillful use of Russian folk-material within a drama that shows no strong sense of direction or sympathetic identification with any of the characters (that would have to wait until *Eugene Onegin* and *The Maid of Orléans*). Although certain passages were to find no happier home in his next complete opera, *The Oprichnik*, Tchaikovsky eventually salvaged several of *The Voyevoda*'s best numbers in the context of *Swan Lake*. He did the same with the music of *Undine*, a watery fairytale set to music in the first eight months of 1869. It was never produced, although three numbers were performed in concert and the love duet of the nymph and her knight attained immortality as voiced by violin and cello in *Swan Lake's* Act Two Pas de Deux.

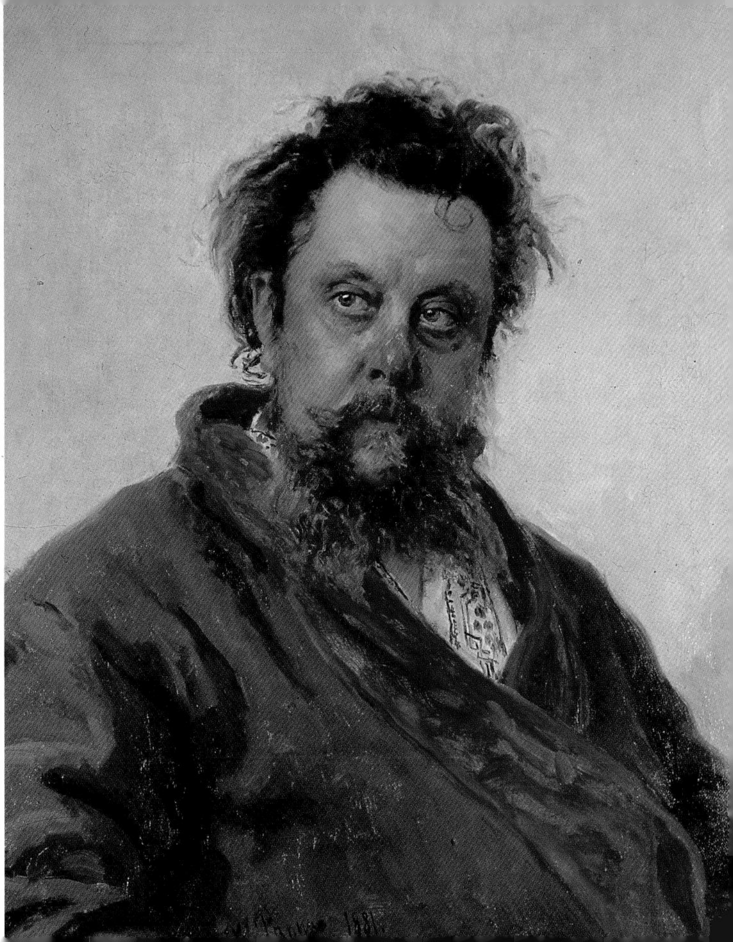

The 'Mighty Handful': Mussorgsky, portrait by Repin (1881) (AKG)

During the two years in which he worked on his opera, affairs of the heart touched Tchaikovsky closely, the first verging on tragedy, the second a comedy. In June 1867, finances permitted only a stringently economical trip to Vyborg and Hapsal (on the Baltic, in what is now the republic of Estonia). There it became obvious that Vera Davydova, sister-in-law of his own sister Sasha, was in love with him. For the first time in his life, Tchaikosky had to come to terms with his own incapacity to feel anything in return, despite the best intentions. He tried to argue his way out of the situation – which he must have half-encouraged – in a letter to Sasha that August:

> *I am bound to suffer some degree of torment precisely because I am grateful to her and do most sincerely love her. Please assure her that my heart has always responded to her with the warmest friendship and gratitude – in case she is in any doubt on the matter, which would surprise me. As to my coldness, which so distresses her – it has a number of causes, of which the main one is that I love her as a sister but because of the pressure of various social conventions our relationship cannot be sincere; this sets up a wall, as it were, between us, through which we can have no direct relationship with each other. Apart from that there are all manner of psychological subtleties which probably only a Tolstoy or a Thackeray could analyse properly.*

Tchaikovsky attempted to make amends for his lack of true feeling by dedicating his Op.2 piano piece, *Souvenir de Hapsal*, to Vera. But this was by no means the end of her unhappy infatuation, and the situation was to be repeated, with disastrous consequences, in 1877, the year of *Eugene Onegin*.

Quite unique in Tchaikovsky's life, on the other hand, was the *affaire Artôt.* Tchaikovsky first met the Belgian soprano Désirée Artôt when she came to St. Petersburg as the star of an Italian opera company in the spring of 1868, and he came to know her better while he was providing recitatives and a chorus for her benefit performance of Auber's *Le Domino Noir* the following season. (Auber's pleasing *opéra comique* has recently been recorded, after over a century of neglect, with some of Tchaikovsky's contributions added for extra flavor.) Tchaikovsky chose to present his relationship with the prima donna in one way to his father, another to Modest. He obviously felt that Ilya expected him to marry soon when he wrote to him in January 1869 that this was exactly what he and Artôt had in mind, but the obstacles he puts in the way have a ring familiar from the letter about Vera sent to Sasha. Désirée's mother objected, he told his father, and his own friends, Nikolay Rubinstein especially, were 'making the most strenuous efforts to ensure that I do not carry out my proposed plan to get married':

> *They say that if I become the husband of a famous singer I will play the wretched role of my wife's husband, that's to say that I will have to travel all over Europe with her and that I will have to live at her expense, that I will get out of the habit of working and will not have the chance to do any.*

And he added that he believed this himself. It seems unlikely that the relationship was ever anything more than the intense admiration of the creative artist (and homosexual) for the diva, but in any case its 'termination' caused Tchaikovsky few of the usual heartaches. Later that year he confided flippantly to Modest:

The Artôt business has resolved itself in the most amusing way. In Warsaw she has fallen in love with the baritone Padilla, who was the object of her ridicule when she was here, and is marrying him! What of the lady? You would need to know the details of our relationship to have any idea of how funny this denouement is.

That is the last we hear of the subject, though there is one interesting footnote: the daughter of the soprano and the baritone, Lola Artôt de Padilla, also became a singer and went on to sing Octavian in the first Berlin performance of Strauss's *Der Rosenkavalier*. Rumor also has it that Désirée is behind the unspecified program of Tchaikovsky's next tone poem, *Fatum* (a 'feeble thing', he called it, but all three main ideas are strong and memorable; only their working-out is weak) and, more likely, that his quotation of a French chansonette in the slow movement of the First Piano Concerto, Op.23, was to serve as fond remembrance of a favorite number in her repertoire.

Far more fruitful, in the long term, was his surprising friendship with Balakirev. The dogmatic leading light of the Five was enjoying new-found favor in his appointment as the conductor of the St. Petersburg RMS Concerts – those very establishment events which his own Free Music Society had opposed so vigorously – when Tchaikovsky made his acquaintance in Moscow in early 1868. Balakirev's popularity was not to last long; after losing the RMS post in 1869, he turned his attention back to his own Free Music School, but his 1871 series of concerts spelled financial disaster. He took on a clerical position in a railway freight station and besides, as Rimsky-Korsakov wrote in his autobiography, 'A great moral change was going on within him: this great unbeliever had turned religious mystic and fanatic.'

A nineteenth-century painting of Romeo and Juliet, *Act V, Scene 4 by William Hatherell (Bristol Art Museum & Art Gallery/Bridgeman)*

All this, however, happened some time after the two-year period during which he guided Tchaikovsky towards his first true masterpiece, *Romeo and Juliet*.

Tchaikovsky proved just how close he was moving to the ideals of the 'mighty handful' with his 1868 piano-duet arrangements of fifty Russian folksongs, with private acknowledgment (gratefully received) to Balakirev's pioneering work in a field which Tchaikovsky simply elaborated, though with good taste. Then there were the two performances of *Fatum*, the first in Moscow on February 27, 1869, the second conducted by Balakirev himself in St. Petersburg just over a month later, which Tchaikovsky dedicated to the 'father of the Five', only to receive a fair but all the same devastating criticism from Balakirev. Their relationship survived the blow. Tchaikovsky responded swiftly:

> *I admit I was not in raptures about your review but I was not at all offended and in my heart I respected the sincere directness which is one of the most attractive features of your musical personality. I will, of course, not withdraw the dedication but I hope to write something a bit better for you one day.*

That day came sooner rather than later. Balakirev visited Moscow in the summer of 1869, and although Tchaikovsky found certain aspects of his personality disagreeable – 'his narrowness of view … as well as the stubbornness with which he sticks to his enthusiasms' – he respected his integrity. When the bald outline of the new fantasy overture that he had begun to sketch on October 7 failed to inspire him, he took due note of Balakirev's detailed instructions. The older composer told him how the strict framework that he had forced on his own *King Lear* Overture had brought forth ideas, and he gave Tchaikovsky his own selection of events from the chosen subject, Shakespeare's *Romeo and Juliet*.

Tchaikovsky took heed. In November he replied:

My overture is getting on quite quickly; the greater part has already been sketched out and a considerable part of what you advised me to do has been done. In the first place, the layout is yours: *the introduction portraying the friar {Laurence}, the fight – Allegro {Balakirev had even written out scurrying string music for sword-clashes}, and love – the second subject; and secondly, the modulations are yours.*

He confided only fragments of the principal themes, and for us it is fascinating to note that Balakirev criticized the Friar Laurence theme: 'Here there ought to be something like Liszt's chorales ... with an ancient catholic character resembling that of Orthodox church music.' That is more or less what we have in the memorably solemn wind chords at the start of the fantasy overture as we know it, and intriguingly the original version which Tchaikovsky revised, taking up Balakirev's suggestion rather belatedly in the summer following the first performance on March 28, 1870, still exists (and has been recorded) to show us how much weaker and less atmospheric Tchaikovsky's original friar theme certainly is. Other gains of the 1870 revision include the tightening-up of the development to bring the new 'Friar Laurence' theme unexpectedly but thrillingly into the fighting: it peals out on trumpets at the central climax.

One crucial element of the work, of course, had never been in doubt – the love theme. 'The second D flat tune is simply *delightful*,' Balakirev wrote in that same crucial letter. 'I play it often, and I want very much to kiss you for it. Here are tenderness and the sweetness of love.' The element of poignant regret in this great melody, first heard on cor anglais and strings, surely comes from the element of autobiography, that sense of 'unlucky in love', which Tchaikovsky would discuss obliquely in his later correspondence with Nadezhda von Meck. The tender music of the star-crossed lovers is Tchaikovsky's first deep sounding of the personal note which was to be taken up in love scenes to come. As for Balakirev, having further prompted Tchaikovsky – unsuccessfully, as it turned out – in the direction of a fantastical cantata, with Berlioz's magical orchestration as an example, he retreated from the scene, only to make a dramatic reappearance as the imaginative sponsor of another imposing work, the *Manfred* Symphony, Op.58, in the 1880s.

The subjective romanticism which we tend to identify as Tchaikovsky's strongest characteristic also surfaces in his first set of songs, or (to give them their proper Russian title) romances, completed in 1869. It is possible to accuse Tchaikovsky of generalizing emotions in his song output, but he did after all tend to choose texts of a vaguely amorous nature. At least the prevailing theme of lost or unrequited love seems to have encouraged a sincere response, and in three of this famous Op.6 set – 'Do not believe, my friend', 'Not a word' and the best-loved of all his romances, 'None but the lonely heart' – the contours of the vocal line are utterly distinctive, fascinating precursors of the style that was to flourish in *Eugene Onegin*. In the First String Quartet of 1871, on the other hand, he played cool in his first conscious tribute to Mozart and the classical tradition: after all, there was little authentically Russian precedent for the subtler art of chamber music. To us the rococo twists and the over-careful formal balance of the work often seem cold, though we can still understand the enthusiasm of audiences at the time for the ever-popular Andante cantabile, which as we have seen takes for its chaste principal theme a folksong noted down at Kamenka.

Lament though he might to Modest in later years that audiences didn't want to know anything else of his but this Andante cantabile, Tchaikovsky recorded in his diary for 1876 that he was 'never more flattered in my life, nor was my pride as a composer so stirred as when Leo Tolstoy, sitting beside me listening to the Andante of my First Quartet, dissolved in tears'. This meeting with the author of *War and Peace* and *Anna Karenina* was not, in some other respects, the happy occasion it should have been, since Tolstoy talked with a layman's arrogance about music (making the unanswerable remark that 'Beethoven lacked talent'). But Tchaikovsky remained in complete harmony with Tolstoy's 'colossal talent', and the writer only helped to confirm a conviction which he already held, which he carried out in practice for the rest of his life, and which still holds good today:

He has convinced me that the artist who works not in response to an inner stimulus but with a careful calculation of the effect *which he will achieve, who does violence to his talent with the aim of pleasing, and who forces himself to satisfy the public, that such a man is not truly an artist, that his works will not last, that his success is ephemeral.*

For Tchaikovsky, Tolstoy remained 'the greatest writer in the world, past or present' because of his tremendous pity for the bad behavior of his characters. 'Tolstoy never has villains; he loves and pities all his characters equally, everything that they do is a consequence of the general constraints from which they suffer, of their naive egoism, their feebleness, their insignificance,' he wrote to the Grand Duke Konstantin in 1885; for this reason, he continued, he preferred Tolstoy to Dickens, another favorite author of his. One imagines he would have made a wonderful operatic figure out of Natasha, the emotionally impulsive and sympathetically characterized heroine of *War and Peace*, but that task had to wait until Prokofiev, another fervent reader of the novel, set it selectively to music half a century after Tchaikovsky's death.

The other giant of Russian literature, Dostoevsky, provoked a more wary response from the composer in his younger, more febrile days. Reading *The Brothers Karamazov* in 1879, he was so moved by one scene that 'it shook me with sobbing and an attack of hysteria'. Two years later, he was still apparently struggling with the novel, anxious to finish it and announcing to Modest: 'Dostoyevsky is a writer of genius but I don't like him. The more I read of him, the more he gets me down.' The comparatively subdued character studies of Turgenev gave him much pleasure during his Moscow Conservatoire days, but by the mid-1880s he had virtually deserted him – for no reason, he wrote, that he could make out – in favor of Tolstoy. Turgenev, incidentally, was in the audience at the première of the First String Quartet, though whether it affected him as deeply then as it did Tolstoy five years later is not recorded.

The estate at Kamenka provided further inspiration – though not, this time, a folksong – in the summer following the March 1871 première of the First String Quartet. Sasha furnished rooms for Tchaikovsky away from the rest of the busy household, though this did not exclude him from the family fun and games which he found so necessary. Far from it; this summer Uncle Petya involved three of the

Davydov children – Tatyana aged ten, Vera aged eight and the seven-year-old Anna
– as well as his brother Modest in a home-made ballet. The details were passed on to
one of the two Davydov sons yet to be born, Yury, who depicts Tchaikovsky 'red in
the face, wet with perspiration as he sang the tune', having choreographed the entire
thing himself. The subject was none other than *Swan Lake* – with wooden toy swans
– though it is doubtful if any of the music eventually went into the ballet, the
outline of which Tchaikovsky did not discuss until 1875.

*The Davidovs at Kramenka,
1880. Tchaikovsky's sister
Sasha and her husband Lev
are seated center (Lebrecht)*

After this domestic idyll, he moved on to the country estate of Nikolay Kondratyev, a rumbustious fellow lawyer, and – before returning to independence in a Moscow flat of his own away from Nikolay Rubinstein – he visited the quieter, if less lavishly appointed, Usovo home of Vladimir Shilovsky, now a close friend. How close remains open to question, but they were intimate enough for the wealthy and consumptive Shilovsky to summon Tchaikovsky to Paris the previous June, having persuaded his impecunious friend to travel at his expense and to nurse him through his convalescence at a German spa town (this orderly existence came to an end when the sudden onset of the Franco-Prussian War forced them to leave). At the end of that year, too, Tchaikovsky enjoined his brother Modest to absolute secrecy about the month he was going to spend with Shilovsky in Nice. Whatever the circumstances – and Tchaikovsky certainly did not like being financially dependent on Shilovsky – he was to spend portions of the next five summers at Usovo.

It was at Kamenka, though, that Tchaikovsky carried out his best creative work. He wrote the first act of his next opera, *The Oprichnik*, there and the following year, 1872, Kamenka's healing atmosphere encouraged him to make a start on his Second Symphony, Op.17, after a season of exhausting duties at the Moscow Conservatoire. He completed the symphony in November, drained but this time triumphant. 'I think it's my best work as regards perfection of form', he wrote to Modest. He ended the year crowned with laurels from the Mighty Handful on a Christmas-time visit to St. Petersburg: 'I played the finale at a soirée at Rimsky-Korsakov's, and the assembled company nearly tore me to shreds in their rapture.' That was quite understandable, given their nationalist principles: in his Finale, Tchaikovsky takes a Ukrainian folksong, 'The Crane', heralds it grandly much as Mussorgsky was to do with 'The Great Gate of Kiev' in his *Pictures from an Exhibition*, and then sets in train a string of leg-kicking arrangements of the theme. The method, in which the tune remains the same but the orchestration and sometimes the harmonies around it are altered, has its roots in a short but colorful orchestral work by Glinka, *Kamarinskaya*, which Tchaikovsky fêted with the immortal remark that all Russian music was in it 'just as all the oak is in the acorn'.

This was clearly the best movement as far as Tchaikovsky was concerned; he even gave his symphony the subtitle *The Crane* (and not *Little Russian*, a later nickname by his friend Kashkin which refers to the Ukraine in terms its people have since considered offensive). But he seems to have found the ambitious symphonic scheme of the original first movement to his liking at the time. It was not until the winter of 1879–80 that he changed his mind and virtually rewrote it after the Introduction, providing a lively new first subject, closer to Beethoven in its rhythmic energy than anything else in his symphonies, and cutting down on the lyricism. 'This movement has now come out compact, nice and short, and not difficult,' he wrote to his fellow composer Taneyev. 'If anything deserved the description *impossible* it was the first movement in its original form. My God! It was difficult, noisy, incoherent and muddled.' Difficult and noisy the original may be – and the revised version we usually hear today makes fewer demands on the orchestra – but Tchaikovsky had no need to be ashamed of its structure; a recording and the occasional live performance give us a chance to make up our own minds. In 1880 Tchaikovsky left the Andante as it was (the spry outer portions are reworked from the discarded *Undine*), tightened up the Scherzo and made one judicious cut in the Finale. In either version the Second Symphony, for all the shades of Russian melancholy in it, remains the most refreshing alternative to the autobiographical soul-searching of the last three symphonies.

If work on the Second Symphony had been only marginally less stressful than the composition of its predecessor, Tchaikovsky found nothing but pleasure in his next three projects. He renewed his working friendship with Ostrovsky when the playwright was given free rein to fashion a Bolshoi extravaganza for singers, actors and dancers, *The Snow Maiden*. In March 1873 Tchaikovsky was commissioned to provide nineteen numbers for this magical tale of the girl whose icy heart is melted by the rays of love, and the score was ready by the beginning of April. The task had proved anything but tiresome. Tchaikovsky later wrote to Nadezhda von Meck:

> The Snow Maiden ... *is one of my favourite children. It was a marvellous spring; my spirits were high, as always at the approach of summer and three months of freedom. I liked Ostrovsky's play and I wrote the music in three weeks, without any effort. I think that you can feel in this music the happy, spring-like mood which possessed me at the time.*

The same 'spring-like mood' also possessed Rimsky-Korsakov when he faithfully adapted *The Snow Maiden* as his first successful opera in 1883, and it is a pity for Tchaikovsky's attractive numbers that his contemporary's even more imaginative work has eclipsed both the play and the incidental music in Russia; though even the Rimsky-Korsakov opera, quite inexplicably, is rarely seen in the West.

Financed by the fairly handsome fee for his commission, as well as a better salary for his Conservatoire work, further income from his newly established post as a music critic on *The Russian Gazette* and an advance on royalties for *The Oprichnik* (still to be staged), Tchaikovsky set off again for Western Europe. This time he absorbed the natural wonders of Switzerland as well as the known delights of Paris, although his love affair with Italy was forestalled by a heatwave, and he turned northwards having reached Milan. The real pleasure of the summer, though, was to find himself back in Russia for August and alone at Usovo (Shilovsky had gone to Moscow). He expressed his joy in nature to Modest:

I was in some sort of exalted condition of spiritual bliss, wandering on my own through the woods during the day and, towards evening, across the measureless steppe; at night I sat by the open window listening to the solemn stillness of this isolated place, broken from time to time by vague nocturnal sounds. In the course of these two weeks, without any effort, as though moved by some supernatural force, I wrote the rough draft of the whole of The Tempest.

The subject of Shakespeare's swansong had been suggested to him before work on *The Snow Maiden* intervened by Vladimir Stasov, the great (if partial) art and music critic who now seemed to be taking over the reins of the nationalist school from Balakirev. Again, the program was preordained, though Tchaikovsky found room for the magic of nature he was experiencing at Usovo in the supernatural spell which opens and closes the work, and in the fantastical dialogues of Ariel and Caliban. His lovers are not quite as natural or as innocent as they should be; a hint of sadness in their music provides the inspired, though inappropriate, lyrical link between *Romeo and Juliet* and the forthcoming *Francesca da Rimini*, Op.32.

Rimsky-Korsakov and Stasov adored *The Tempest*, Op.18, though they did not hear it until November 1874; the première had taken place the previous December, and its success spurred Tchaikovsky on to a third, easily written piece, his Second String Quartet, Op.22. 'I regard it as my best work,' he told Modest. 'No other piece has poured forth from me so simply and easily. I wrote it almost at one sitting' (at the end of January 1874). This time the cool, classical world of the First Quartet is almost violently contrasted with a familiar vein of nervous tension which surfaces in the very Russian slow movement. But like its companions in the triumvirate of Tchaikovsky's most effortless compositional year, the Second String Quartet receives few airings today – fewer, certainly, than its predecessor.

Francesca da Rimini: painting by Ary Scheffer, 1835 (Bridgeman)

The new opera that Tchaikovsky had been working on was premièred at last in St. Petersburg on April 24, 1874. Conducted by the masterful if pedantic Eduard Napravnik, an important name in Russian music, *The Oprichnik* was a hit with the public and firmly consolidated Tchaikovsky's reputation – a supreme irony, because he hated it. 'This opera is so bad that I fled from all the rehearsals ... so as not to hear a single note and at the performance I wished the earth would swallow me,' he wrote to Modest. Nor was this the kind of capricious verdict typical of the composer's other judgments, for he remained adamant to the end of his life. It was a good opportunity to revive some of the music from *The Voyevoda*, packed into a darker slice of Russian history: the *oprichnina* was the iron ring formed by Ivan the Terrible in 1565 to fight the power of the boyars, though it turned into a forerunner of the KGB – as Prokofiev and the filmmaker Sergei Eisenstein realized when working on Part Two of *Ivan the Terrible* while Stalin was in power (they nearly lost their lives for the implied link). Tchaikovsky had no such political point to make in adapting Ivan Lazhechnikov's play at a time of relatively liberal tsarist rule; he wanted an operatic pageant, a Russian answer to the grand operas of the then-popular French master of spectaculars Giacomo Meyerbeer, with love-interest to offer some kind of coherent plot.

Nationalist in style, like *The Voyevoda*, *The Oprichnik* is once again no rival to Mussorgsky's *Boris Godunov*, which had finally reached the stage in its complete first version two months earlier. (Tchaikovsky studied the score and found it 'utterly and damnably awful; it is the most vulgar and squalid parody of music'. Like most of his musical colleagues at the time, he saw Mussorgsky's unorthodox and prophetic writing as mere technical barbarity.) Nor should *The Oprichnik*'s passing attractions

The Imperial State Theaters: the Maryinsky in St. Petersburg …

divert our attention from what is undoubtedly Tchaikovsky's first operatic masterpiece, and the best of all his most neglected works, *Vakula the Smith*, Op.14. Tchaikovsky might not have lighted on his most inspired operatic subject yet had it not been for a competition announced by the Petersburg branch of the Russian Musical Society at the end of 1873: all entrants were to set Gogol's short story *Christmas Eve* as an opera. At first he made a mistake about the closing date for entries, which may have helped with the white heat of his initial inspiration; once apprised of the true deadline, which was a year later than he had thought (January 1875, not 1874), he comfortably polished off his operatic fairy tale surrounded by the peaceful charms of Usovo. It won the competition, of course; with friends on the panel of judges, Tchaikovsky could hardly have failed. But as Rimsky-Korsakov pointed out in retrospect, this one incident in the otherwise honorable Tchaikovsky's life where he could have been accused of nepotism did not overshadow the simple fact that his score was infinitely superior to the others submitted.

Vakula the Smith is a delightful opera worthy of a place beside *Eugene Onegin* and *The Queen of Spades*, if only because it shows us the relaxed Tchaikovsky of the later ballets alongside the easy-going nationalist welcomed by Balakirev and company. *Christmas Eve* belongs to Gogol's earliest surviving set of writings from 1831, *Evenings on a farm near Dikanka*, and although this comic genius would go on to startle his readers with the ultimate in bizarre satires like *The Nose*, his early stories are gentle in their irony. Tchaikovsky respected the bouncing humor in those scenes of *Christmas Eve* which lightly touch on the relationship between the witch Solokha and the Devil, but what really interested him was the true feeling of Solokha's son Vakula, the good-hearted smith who obeys the caprices of the vain but likable

... and the Bolshoi in Moscow (Lebrecht)

Oxana and press-gangs the Devil into traveling to St. Petersburg and procuring the pair of royal slippers she requests. *The Slippers* (*Cherevichki*) was, in fact, the title Tchaikovsky gave the opera when he revised it in 1886. For once, the original version is preferable; he made the revision to cut down on the wealth of orchestral detail and make life easier for the singers, and where he added (especially at the end of Act One) he only prolonged the action beyond its charming limits. *Vakula the Smith* deserved to do as well in the West as Rimsky-Korsakov's 1894 setting *Christmas Eve*, which is hardly better than Tchaikovsky's more down-to-earth tale, only different.

Tchaikovsky's own *Christmas Eve* in 1874 turned into a celebrated fiasco when Nikolay Rubinstein asked for a playthrough of his newly completed Piano Concerto. Tchaikovsky had hoped that his friend and guide would be the soloist in the first performance, and all he sought were a few words of advice, since he did not regard himself as a pianist. What he got, after playing through the long and complex first movement, were silence first and invective shortly afterward:

> *It appeared that my concerto was no good at all, that it was unplayable, that some passages were hackneyed, awkward and clumsy beyond redemption, that I had stolen this bit from somewhere and that bit from somewhere, that there were only two or three pages which could stand and the rest would have to be thrown away or completely revised ... I cannot convey the main thing, which is the tone in which all this was said.*

When Tchaikovsky had calmed down sufficiently to face Rubinstein, he was given a more measured ultimatum; if he would make radical alterations at specific points, then Rubinstein would play it. '"I will not revise a single note," I replied, "and I will publish it in exactly the form it is now!" And I did.'

This was the dramatic story as Tchaikovsky told it to Nadezhda von Meck several years later. And yet, although it was the German conductor and pianist Hans von Bülow who gave the successful first performance on his American tour the following October and who became the dedicatee, Rubinstein was soon reconciled to the dazzling merits of the First Piano Concerto, Op.23. Having conducted the Moscow première (still grudgingly, one assumes), he took on the solo role in February 1878. 'I was quite sure he would play it splendidly,' Tchaikovsky told Madame von Meck in quite a different vein. 'The concerto was really written for him and it counts upon his immense powers as a virtuoso.' Perhaps Rubinstein had not realized, at that first audition, quite how skillfully Tchaikovsky pitches his epic first-movement battle between heavyweight soloist and orchestra. This movement, prefaced by the famous, never-to-be-heard again melody, remains a unique adventure in the concerto repertoire; not that the varied charms of the Andantino or the effectiveness of the racy Finale should be underestimated either.

Less striking is the Third Symphony, Op.29, premièred at around the same time, where Tchaikovsky's classical discipline sometimes takes the upper hand. Foursquare, plainly dressed themes in the outer movements, including a rather clipped Polonaise which led to the English nicknaming the symphony 'Polish', contrast with genuine charm and melodies from the heart in the central sequence (three movements rather than the usual two). 'So far as I can see, this symphony has no particularly inventive ideas but in terms of technique it is a step forward', Tchaikovsky wrote to Rimsky-Korsakov, whose own Third Symphony of the same year (1875) is a far colder exercise in musicianly correctness.

For all the breath of academic chill that can occasionally be detected in the Third Symphony, or for that matter in a third String Quartet, Op.30, where he feared he had written himself out, the next work that Tchaikovsky completed must have reassured him that his usual compositional fertility had not deserted him. In the summer of 1876 he set about orchestrating his first ballet, *Swan Lake*, Op.20, the scenario for which he had settled upon at the beginning of the previous year in conjunction with two artistically minded drinking companions, the stage manager of the Bolshoi Ballet Vladimir Begichev and Vasily Geltser, one of the company's leading dancers. 'I have taken on this task partly because of the money, partly because I have wanted to try my hand at this sort of music for a long time,' Tchaikovsky told Rimsky-Korsakov. Thereafter, hardly any correspondence or information about the ballet's genesis survives, though that delightful summer entertainment at Kamenka certainly played its part, and the original storyline of the swan-princess under the spell of the evil magician Rothbart and the prince who falls in love with her blends German and Russian legends to imaginative ends.

It was a bold experiment. Tchaikovsky drew infinite variety from the standard forms of dance: you only have to look and listen to many and supple waltzes, the first and most famous of which is in itself a parade of inspired ideas in 3/4 time to match the finest specimens of Johann Strauss. His real achievement, though, was to hold the narrative thread between set pieces, with dramatic emphasis on the drama of the Second Act – in the two numbers (11 and 12) before the Divertissement – and the final catastrophe of the short but genuinely tragic Act Four, where the well-known swan theme is taken to its extreme point of development. As far as Tchaikovsky was

*The Swan Princess – painting by the
turn-of-the-century artist Vrubel
(Lebrecht)*

concerned when he wrote *Swan Lake*, this was something completely new in ballet; he had not yet encountered the French composer Delibes' *Coppélia* and *Sylvia*, and he was all too familiar with the any-purpose hackwork of Minkus and Drigo, whose scores accompanied the gems of Russian choreography and are still laboriously preserved (for the sake of the dancing) in the Bolshoi and Kirov repertoires. Unfortunately, *Swan Lake* was not to be graced with the kind of production it deserved. The première on March 4, 1877, a benefit-night for the prima ballerina Pelageya Karpakova, featured choreography of breathtaking ineptitude by one Julius Reisinger (who borrowed what he did not so lamely invent), threadbare sets and costumes pieced together from other productions, and shoddy orchestral playing. The ballet was not revived until two years after Tchaikovsky's death, when the highly successful choreographer of *The Sleeping Beauty* and *The Nutcracker*, Marius Petipa, worked on Modest Tchaikovsky's revised plot scenario; apart from the false resurrection from death of Odette and the Prince at the end, it is a vast improvement and deserves its lasting popularity.

Even given the circumstances of 1877, though, the critics ought to have been a little more perceptive about the music. Golden hindsight award goes to the writer who found 'Mr. Tchaikovsky's usual shortcoming: a poverty of creative fantasy and, in consequence of this, thematic and melodic monotony'. This was nothing new, of course. Exactly two years earlier, an opera which was to have the greatest influence on Tchaikovsky had opened in Paris, to mostly scathing reviews. 'I do not mean to say that there are not what are called themes in M. Bizet's music' opined *Le Siècle*. 'Unfortunately, as a rule, they are anything but original and they lack distinction … He thinks too much and does not feel enough, and his inspirations, even when most

Scene from the unsuccessful Moscow première of Swan Lake, 1877 *(Lebrecht)*

happy, lack sincerity and truth …' That was what the press thought (or, some say, was paid to think) about *Carmen*. Tchaikovsky was a better judge – 'I am convinced that in ten years or so Carmen will be the most popular opera in the world' – but by the time he wrote that, in 1879, the tide of opinion had turned.

It was at the beginning of 1876, when he spent a month traveling in France with Modest, that he first saw *Carmen* in Paris. 'Rarely have I seen my brother so deeply moved by a performance in the theatre', Modest later wrote of this, the first successful staging in Paris since the original débâcle and Bizet's untimely death shortly afterwards. In later years Tchaikovsky was to become obsessed by the fateful relationship of Carmen and Don José and Bizet's music retained its influence on him to the last, obviously so in *The Queen of Spades* and the 'Pathétique' Symphony, Op.74. But what fascinated him was the very French elegance with which Bizet treated a subject from contemporary life:

> … *indeed I know of nothing in music which has a better right to stand for the element which I call* the pretty, le joli. *It is fascinating and delightful from beginning to end; there are plenty of piquant harmonies and completely new combinations of sounds, but that is not the exclusive aim; Bizet is an artist who pays due tribute to his age and his times but he is fired with true inspiration.*

He envied the French their lightness of touch and their freshness, so long as it was governed by inspiration. That was true, he thought, of Massenet's Eastern fantasy *Le Roi de Lahore* – 'Damn it all, these Frenchmen have such taste, such style' – but not his *Manon*; he found most of Gounod's operas mediocre except for *Faust* and *Romeo et*

Richard Wagner (AKG)

'The Wagner-Theater in Bayreuth after its completion' – 1873 *woodcut after a painting by Sauter (AKG)*

Juliette, and nearly fainted at the power of Meyerbeer's *Robert le Diable* but favored the negative judgment of future generations when it came to *L'Africaine.* Yet he could never speak too highly of the Delibes ballets and he would never have written *Swan Lake,* he said, had he known *Sylvia* at the time.

Tchaikovsky's love for this mythological ballet also eclipsed what might, for many other music lovers, have been the listening event of a lifetime. In August 1876 he set out (with the piano score of *Sylvia* among his possessions, newly purchased in Paris) for the theater which Richard Wagner had commanded to be built for the staging of his music-dramas in the small Bavarian town of Bayreuth. Tchaikovsky came to the first-ever complete, four-day presentation of *Der Ring des Nibelungen* not as an ardent Wagnerian but in order to discharge his final duties as music critic of *The Russian Gazette*. He had already made up his critical mind about Wagner's true vocation, which he believed to be as a symphonist; in his stage works, he thought, Wagner 'subjects the singer to a whole orchestral horde, which not only deprives the stage characters of their supremacy but also drowns them' – at least after *Lohengrin*, which he later judged 'the crowning glory of Wagner's achievement'. So he was out of sympathy with Wagner's attempts to fuse music and drama into one theatrical entity, and seeing *The Ring* only confirmed his beliefs. He confessed in his *Gazette* articles, written in Nuremberg after he had left Bayreuth, that 'it is my own fault, I willingly admit, that I have not yet risen to a proper understanding of this music', and added that his final impression was

> ... *a confused recollection of many striking beauties, especially those of a symphonic character, which is very odd, since least of all was Wagner trying to write a symphonic opera; I came away with amazed respect for the composer's enormous talent and for his unprecedented technical resources; I came away in doubt about the validity of Wagner's view of opera; I came away quite exhausted, but at the same time wishing to continue my study of this music, the most complex that has ever been written.*

To Modest he was more blunt: 'Finally on Thursday it all came to an end and with the final chords of *Götterdämmerung* I felt as if I had been liberated from captivity.'

Yet even if, like Rossini, Tchaikovsky had found 'lovely moments, but awful quarters of an hour' in *The Ring*, it had a powerful effect on his next composition which he duly acknowledged.

On his way to Paris earlier that summer, Tchaikovsky had found himself absorbed by the Fourth Canto of Dante's *Inferno* and the character depicted therein of Francesca da Rimini, murdered along with her lover Paolo by her furious husband and condemned to hell for her adulterous passion. When he set to work on the subject back in Moscow for the next academic year, Tchaikovsky could not help making his framework – Dante's descent to hell with the shade of Virgil and the hellish whirlwind that surrounds them – rife with Wagnerian elements. The dark brass chordings come straight from the world of *Die Walküre*, as Tchaikovsky admitted to his disciple and fellow composer Sergei Taneyev in 1878. 'Isn't it odd that I should have submitted to the influence of a work of art that in general is extremely antipathetic to me?' he added.

At the heart of the whirlwind in *Francesca da Rimini*, Op.32, though, is the plaintive portrait of a love forbidden which is pure Tchaikovsky, and his most autobiographical piece of writing yet. He headed his scheme with the most famous of quotations from Dante – 'nessun maggior dolore, che ricordarsi del tempo felice nella miseria' ('there is no greater sorrow than to recall a time of happiness in the midst of misery') – which he had already quoted to Modest in the personal context of the melancholy which was oppressing him during a deadly few weeks at Vichy earlier in the summer of 1876. He had already pinpointed the roots of a malaise that was returning with increasing frequency the previous year, knowing that only Modest (who was also homosexual) could understand them. The missing words in square brackets below have been conjectured by the sympathetic archivist from the Tchaikovsky museum at Klin, Alexandra Orlova, but the gist remains perfectly obvious:

It is a fact that {my inclinations} create an impassable gulf between the majority of people and myself. They impart to my character a host of features – a sense of alienation, fear of others, timidity, excessive shyness, mistrustfulness – which make me more and more unsociable.

By the time of his return from Bayreuth, the pressure had become unbearable. Work on an occasional piece to show Russia's support of Montenegro and Serbia in their war against the Turks, the *Marche Slave*, Op.31 (based on three Serbian tunes, colorfully scored, and noisily capped by the Russian national anthem), turned his attention to external events; *Francesca* drove him back to his own predicament. The correspondence with Modest becomes more explicit:

I am now going through a very critical period of my life. I will go into more detail later, but for now I will simply tell you: I have decided to get married. It is unavoidable. I must do it, not just for myself but for you as well, and for Tolya, and Sasha, and all those I love ... I think that for both of us our dispositions are the greatest and most insuperable obstacle to happiness and we must fight our natures to the best of our ability.

Modest protested the notion of marriage and the deceit involved. Tchaikovsky's replies attempt a random self-justification:

> *... you say that I mustn't give a damn about* qu'en dira-t-on! *That's true only up to a point. There are those who cannot hold me in contempt for my vices simply because they started to love me before they suspected that my reputation is, in fact, ruined. For example, Sasha is one such! I know that she has* guessed everything *and that she forgives everything. Many people whom I love or respect regard me in the same way. Surely you realize how painful it is for me to know that people* pity and forgive me when, in truth, I am not guilty of anything ... *And, anyway, I don't have an iron will by any means, and after writing to you, I gave into the power of my natural inclinations about three times ... Whatever happens, I am not going to put a* millstone *around my neck. I will only embark on a lawful or unlawful liaison with a woman if I have completely assured my peace and freedom. But I still have nothing definite in view as yet.*

Nor did an opportunity present itself immediately. When it did, that same shortsightedness with regard to the unlucky partner's feelings would contribute to the near-fatal consequences.

In the meantime, the crisis and Tchaikovsky's misanthropy temporarily abated. His next work, the *Variations on a Rococo Theme*, Op.33, for cello and orchestra, begun at the end of 1876, could not have been further removed from the personal hell of *Francesca da Rimini*, and it reflects his cherished belief in the spirit of Mozart as consolation and escape from the nervous spirit of his age. In less than masterly hands, the technical difficulties for the soloist can seem disproportionate to the miniaturist scale. Yet when the cellist who commissioned the work, Eduard Fitzenhagen, cut a variation and re-ordered the sequence, he did so not because he found the writing problematic but simply to highlight his singing tone in the D minor variation (the only one in the work which might hint at Tchaikovsky's melancholy). Fitzenhagen's version is the one we usually hear, though since the composer's original thoughts have been published and taken up by cellists such as Steven Isserlis, there is no good reason for it to remain so.

Nadezhda von Meck (AKG)

Other paid commissions during the same period must have seemed of little importance to Tchaikovsky, but out of them developed the strangest of relationships and one of the most extraordinary correspondences in the history of music. It was at this time that Nadezhda Filaretovna von Meck entered his life. She heard of Tchaikovsky's financial difficulties through her 'house-musician', the violinist Josef Kotek, who had been a devoted pupil of the composer's at the Conservatoire. Through Kotek she commissioned from Tchaikovsky several transcriptions of his own works for violin and piano, handsomely paid. The transcriptions did not continue for long, but Tchaikovsky's need of what he described to his benefactress as *'contemptible metal'* to pay off his debts certainly did. Time and again in the 1,200 letters that followed he makes heartfelt reassurances to the effect that finances are not the motivating force in their friendship, and the remarkable range of his confidences leave us in no doubt of how much Tchaikovsky needed his 'beloved friend'.

Guilelessly, too, he elected Madame von Meck as his accomplice in the Fourth Symphony he had started in March 1877 and which he finished sketching by the end of May, the time at which the correspondence took its crucial turn. *'Our* symphony' he called it when working on the orchestration the following year, and he did not lightly vouchsafe an answer to her question as to whether the symphony had a precise program: 'For the first time in my life I have had to recast my musical ideas and musical images in words and phrases.' This is enough to prove that Tchaikovsky did not compose his most important symphony so far to a preordained program. Yet at the same time his attempt to articulate the moods behind the notes deserves to be taken seriously. The fierce horn and bassoon fanfare which hammers away at the start

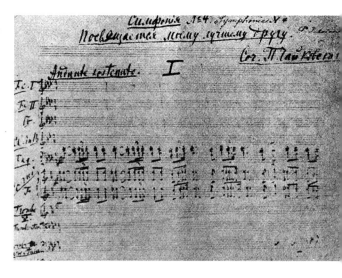

The opening fanfare of the Fourth Symphony, with Tchaikovsky's dedication to his 'beloved friend' (Nadezhda von Meck) (Lebrecht)

of the Fourth Symphony, Op.36, was 'Fate, that inexorable force which prevents our aspirations to happiness from reaching their goal, which jealously ensures that our well-being and peace are not complete and unclouded, which hangs over our head like the sword of Damocles'; the lamenting main subject of the first movement was 'the joyless, hopeless feeling' becoming 'ever more powerful and fierce', while the limping waltz which follows and which gradually brightens represented 'a sweet and tender dream appearing', a vision which is rudely interrupted by the fate-fanfare. 'So life is a constant alternation between grim reality and evanescent visions and dreams of happiness.' The second movement, he continued, was an attempt to capture a melancholy evening mood and 'the sweet sadness of burying oneself in the past'. The startling effect of rushing pizzicato strings in the Scherzo – inspired, surely by Delibes' celebrated pizzicato variation in *Sylvia* – sketched 'the elusive images which flash across one's imagination when one has had a little wine to drink'; they give way to a short wind serenade – 'roistering peasants' – and abrupt brass ('in the distance a military parade goes by'). For his Finale, Tchaikovsky seems to have heeded Tolstoy's advice to 'go among the common people and see how they know to enjoy themselves', though his attempt to shrug off the returning blows of fate ('one can live despite everything') rings a little hollow. Even so, the account seems to confirm the underlying logic of this symphony, which is so much more than a long, *Francesca*-like symphonic poem (first movement) with three short pieces fortuitously attached that Taneyev seems to have thought it was. It is hard to argue with Tchaikovsky's verdict to his patroness that,'I think this symphony is something out of the ordinary, that it is the best thing I have done so far'. He could not have completed it, he continued, but for her.

The only thing Tchaikovsky could not discuss with Nadezhda von Meck was his homosexuality. He came close when she asked him if he had known 'non-Platonic' love. 'Yes and no' was the answer.

If we put the question in a different way and ask whether I have known complete happiness in love then the answer is No, no and no again. In any case the question is answered in my music. If you were to ask me whether I understand the full force, the immeasurable power of this feeling I would answer Yes, yes and yes again *and I would say yet again that my repeated efforts to express in music the torments and, at the same time, the bliss of love have themselves been efforts lovingly made.*

His correspondent might have said much the same, had she been honest. Her marriage to Karl von Meck, a man eleven years her senior who had made his money as a builder of railways, had not been a fulfilled one; it has been suggested that the revelation of her affair with her husband's secretary, and of the resultant child, caused his sudden death in 1875. Perhaps this was why she decided to conduct her passionate friendship with Tchaikovsky solely through correspondence, with only the occasional inadvertent, wordless meeting during their thirteen-year relationship.

Alexander Pushkin (AKG)

This whitest of white 'marriages' could not have suited Tchaikovsky better at this crucial point in his life. Its black counterpart unfolded with terrifying swiftness in the spring and summer of 1877. At the beginning of May he received a written declaration of love from one Antonina Milyukova, a former student at the Conservatoire, and he replied counseling restraint. Then he forgot all about the incident. By the time a second letter arrived from the lady, more unbridled than the first, he was working at white heat on a new opera based on Pushkin's great novel in verse *Eugene Onegin*. The subject, which had been suggested to him earlier that month by the singer Lavrovskaya, caught his imagination partly because this would be an opera peopled with real, feeling human beings (like *Carmen*) and not with exotic cardboard cutouts (like *Aida*), but especially because he was 'in love with' Pushkin's heroine, the seventeen-year old Tatyana, and was obsessed by the scene in which she writes a love letter to the cold, aloof Onegin. This was his starting point, and the scene into which he poured inspired themes of painful yearning enough to furnish half an opera. He was not thinking of Antonina Milyukova as he started work on it, but the fact that her second letter reached him at a time when he was beginning to confuse art and creation with real life marked a decisive turning point. He thought he had behaved worse than Onegin – whose rejection of Tatyana, so brusque in the novel, he turned into a warm and sincere avowal to love her in a brotherly way – and, mistaking the coincidence for fate, agreed to visit Antonina in her own home. The circumstances of their engagement show just how self-absorbed in his frenzy Tchaikovsky must have been. To his friend Kashkin, he explained (my emphases):

At our first meeting I told her that I could not return her love, but that she inspired in me a genuine liking for her. She answered that any sympathetic response on my part was precious to her and that she could be content with that, or something like that.

Eugene Onegin – *the duel scene (Lebrecht)*

P·TSCHAIKOWSKY - ONEGHIN

He made a clearer statement of intent to Nadezhda von Meck:

God can see that I am filled with the very best intentions towards my partner in life and that if we are unhappy together it will not be my fault. If I am marrying without love it is because circumstances have turned out that way. I have not lied to her or deceived her.

Three days after Tchaikovsky made this confession to his patroness, on July 18, the wedding took place. Even during the ceremony, Tchaikovsky was close to breakdown. The honeymoon could only be worse. He found even conversation unbearable on the train to St. Petersburg; Antonina, according to his account, noticed nothing amiss. 'She has a perpetual expression of complete happiness and contentment. *Elle n'est pas difficile.* She agrees to everything and is content with everything,' he wrote to Anatoly from the Hotel Europa, adding that his nights were spent sleeping soundly, thanks to a dose of valerian. But

left: *Tchaikovsky and his unfortunate bride, Antonia Miljukova, 1877 (AKG)*

right: *Marija Klimentova, the original Tatyana in* Eugene Onegin *(Lebrecht)*

over: *The Russian countryside in summer – a painting by Kuindski, 1879 (AKG)*

apparently at some stage the sexual aspect of the marriage reared its head. Tchaikovsky found his bride physically repulsive, as well as musically insensitive – in spite of her training – and ignorant of his music. He had some respite away from his wife at his sister's home in Kamenka, but it was not enough to soothe a disastrous return to Moscow and a nightmarish visit to meet Antonina's grotesque family. One evening in September, he plunged himself in the icy waters of the Moscow River in the hope that he would die of pneumonia; instead, his already robust health improved as a result of this cold bath. He resumed his narrative to Kashkin. 'Before I made any further attempts like this I realized that I could not continue in such circumstances: I wrote to my brother Anatoly and asked him to send me a telegram on behalf of Napravnik saying that my presence was essential in Petersburg, which he promptly did.' Nikolay Rubinstein and Anatoly formed a joint deputation to tell Antonina the truth about her husband's departure, and were amazed by her blank, smiling response.

Any reunion with Antonina was out of the question. So, too, while tongues wagged, was a return to his duties at the Conservatoire. Joint finances came to the rescue. Nikolay Rubinstein persuaded his colleagues at the Conservatoire to grant Tchaikovsky a well-paid year's sabbatical before his newly appointed duties as Russian delegate to the Paris International Exhibition the following year (as it happened, Tchaikovsky was still under too much stress to take up these duties). Nadezhda von Meck, realizing the vacant position for pride of place in her beloved composer's heart, also stepped in to offer 1,000 roubles, to be followed by a further 6,000 to be paid each year. Her allowance was to continue until 1890, and with it the entire pattern of Tchaikovsky's life dramatically altered.

He now had time and money enough to spend his winters in Europe, predominantly in the south where it was warmest, and his summers surrounded by the peace and quiet of the Russian countryside. His attitude to foreign travels has too often been simplified as shortlived enthusiasm followed rapidly by dissatisfaction and an agonizing homesickness, the typical Russian's craving for mother Russia. Yet every *cri de coeur* he makes for the homeland has its opposite number in a declaration of love for the beauties of Italy; as with so many of Tchaikovsky's statements, the opposite is also true, the roots lie in what he recognized as his most overwhelming characteristic – capriciousness. He remained, as he told Nadezhda von Meck, a 'mass of contradiction' without a philosophy or a religion to guide him.

His second impressions of Italy were very different from his first, made on an abortive trip to review the first Milan performance of Glinka's *A Life for the Tsar* in 1874. The deep depression his catastrophic marriage had left in its wake overshadowed the first part of his trip, with a sympathetic Anatoly as traveling companion, from Clarens to Florence – where the street noises jarred on his shattered nerves. He did, however, revise his opinion of Rome:

> *At every turn one had a different view of the city, dirty, like Moscow, but far more picturesque and richer in historical memories. And then the Colosseum, with the ruins of the palace of Constantine beside it. It is all so majestic, huge and beautiful! I am very glad that I left with such a favourable and unforgettable impression.*

He also found Venice far less melancholy, healed this time by the 'absence of the usual commotion that you get in towns' and much more responsive to treasures such as Canova's mausoleum in the Church of the Frari.

When he returned to Florence in February 1878, this time with the art-loving Modest as an enlightening guide around the galleries, he warmed to the leisurely pace of life there and even mustered the inspiration to write a few piano pieces and the Op.38 Romances. The last of them, *Pimpinella*, is based on the song of an eleven-year-old street singer, Vittorio, whose personality he found captivating. He had also completed the orchestration of the Fourth Symphony (in San Remo, staying with Modest and Modest's young charge Kolya Konradi) and *Eugene Onegin*. Traveling back to Clarens, he began work on his first new major opus since the crisis, the Violin Concerto, Op.35. Although the eventual choice of first dedicatee was to be the Conservatoire virtuoso Leopold Auer, composition of the concerto at Clarens was spurred on by the arrival of Josif Kotek, the violinist who had effected his meeting with his patroness. A letter from Tchaikovsky to Modest makes it clear that he had been in love with Kotek, and if he now no longer felt the same way, there was affection enough to mold the continuous stream of melody which is the Violin Concerto's greatest asset. His next substantial piece, the First Suite, Op.43, is both more singular and indicative of the new directions he felt his orchestral writing had to take – at least for the next few years – after the stressful autobiography of the Fourth Symphony. He wanted 'a good rest from symphonic music', he told Nadezhda von Meck, though his adoption of this new form embraced darkness – in the portentous Introduction which results in nothing more than a severe, academic fugue – as well as the lighter touch of ballet music which Taneyev had scorned as out of place in a true symphony. Contrast is everything in this attractive work, never more striking than in the sequence of darkly lyrical Intermezzo – a true successor to

Tatyana's Letter Scene from Eugene Onegin: *Yelena Prokina in Graham Vick's Glyndebourne production (Catherine Ashmore)*

the slow movement of the Fourth Symphony – and the sugar-plum Marche miniature, an exercise in bright, piquant colors which serves as prototype for the music of *The Nutcracker*.

Summer and early autumn back in Russia brought an accumulation of pressures, not least the disapproval of Nikolay Rubinstein at his final decision to resign from the staff of the Conservatoire (as he could now afford to do) and the refusal of Antonina, whose unhinged state was becoming increasingly obvious, to grant him a divorce. For the winter he returned to Florence, where he stayed in a villa rented for him by Mrs. von Meck with only his loyal manservant Alexey for company; the solitude suited him and, having exhausted the sightseeing itinerary on his earlier visits, he felt free to work.

His new project was his first opera on a non-Russian theme, the life of Joan of Arc as dramatized by Schiller in *The Maid of Orléans*. Tchaikovsky knew (and rather despised) Verdi's early *Giovanna d'Arco* and hoped to do better, but he must have realized that everything he had cherished in bringing *Eugene Onegin* to life would have to fall by the wayside. The disparity of subject matter must have seemed all the greater on his return to Russia in March 1878, when the main attraction was a quiet première for *Onegin* – staged as Tchaikovsky had insisted this 'opera without a future' (or, to give it the composer's preferred title, 'lyric scenes') should be, at the Moscow Conservatoire by students whose youthful credibility was more important than their vocal prowess. Every operatic convention that Tchaikovsky had railed against in his defense of the sincerely written but, he suspected, dramatically deficient tribute to Pushkin turns up in *The Maid of Orléans*: ceremonial processions and grand ensembles, static set-pieces for the principals and emblematic minor characters. Continuing his task of collecting source material in congenial Paris, he was dangerously close to the pernicious influence of Meyerbeer, then the great examplar of grand opera. What really makes Tchaikovsky's sixth opera fascinating to us today, though, is his identification with Joan the martyr and victim. He confided to Modest the reasons for his 'excess of inspiration':

Tchaikovsky in 1878 (AKG)

> *I wailed horribly when I was reading the book which Nadezhda Filaretovna {von Meck} gave me about Joan of Arc and I got to the proceedings of the abjuration and the execution itself (she cried out dreadfully as she was being led to execution and begged them not to burn her). I suddenly felt sorrow and pity for all mankind and had a fit of indescribable melancholy.*

Fortunately Tchaikovsky's personality gets the better of his subject at the last minute: his music ignores the opportunities given by the text for Joan's angelic acceptance into heaven and ends in a welter of tumultuous despair – a despair more powerful than that of Onegin who rails against fate, something closer to the world of the Fourth Symphony. It is the only kind of conclusion for an opera which, however ingeniously scored, sees Tchaikovsky elsewhere resorting to artifice and formula to an alarming degree.

The new-found routine of his Russian months was twice disturbed in 1879. Antonina, referred to in correspondence with Nadezhda von Meck only as 'a certain person', had tracked him down in Moscow and forced him to the realization that divorce was out of the question: 'Evidently nothing on earth is going to shake her out of her delusion that in reality I am in love with her.' Nor was retreat to the usual clutch of country homes without its tensions. He loved the peace and natural beauty of Mrs. von Meck's estate at Simaki but felt uncomfortable at the thought of his patroness's proximity: 'I'm used to regarding N. F. as some distant and unseen good angel,' he told Modest; and a couple of days later he came face to face with her in the woods. The most extraordinary thing about this strangest of relationships is that each had been happy enough to see the other, unacknowledged, at the theater or in public, but now both were overcome with embarrassment. Friendship as they understood it was, however, resumed as usual, and Tchaikovsky seems to have been unperturbed by Mrs. von Meck's bizarre confession of her previous jealousy over his marriage in what amounted to a declaration of love.

For the first time in his life, Tchaikovsky found himself bored staying with his sister and brother-in-law at Kamenka that autumn. 'Today I began to create something, and the boredom vanished as if by magic.' That something was the Second Piano Concerto, Op.44, an aristocratic and expansively cheerful successor to the work which Nikolay Rubinstein had first rejected and later come to love; Tchaikovsky was justified in the tease, when Rubinstein looked like taking up the new concerto, to the effect that 'it's desirable that in this instance the gap between

Richard Chamberlain as Tchaikovsky and Glenda Jackson as a nymphomaniac Antonia in Ken Russell's The Music Lovers *(BFI)*

the denunciation and the performance should be shorter'. In fact it was Taneyev who gave the first Russian performance in May 1882, and he found plenty to criticize: excessive length in the first two movements, far too much solo work for the violin and cello soloists who spin long, lyrical lines to offset the pianist in the second movement. The subsequent cuttings and tamperings of his former pupil, Alexandr Siloti, pleased Tchaikovsky no more than the reordered *Rococo Variations* of Fitzenhagen, though the Siloti version tends to have stuck: a pity, because Tchaikovsky's epic themes need room to breathe in the long first movement. Neither they, the soulful musings of the solo strings nor the sparkling profusion of invention in the Finale are as second-rate as detractors claim. The same is true of the two-movement *Concert Fantasia*, Op.56, written in 1884.

Autobiography remains at bay, too, in Tchaikovsky's next sequence of orchestral works. He used his return to Rome for the winter of 1879–80 to make the drastic revision of his Second Symphony and to absorb some of the local color, including a trumpet call from the barracks near his hotel, into 'an Italian fantasy on folkthemes' along the lines of Glinka's Spanish fantasies. The *Capriccio Italien*, Op.45, is a dashing picture postcard, but Rimsky-Korsakov was to cap what Tchaikovsky described as its 'brilliant and effective' scoring in his *Capriccio Espagnol* eight years later. No such faith in his orchestration, or any other aspect, made Tchaikovsky's task any easier later in the year back at Kamenka as he worked at Nikolay Rubinstein's request on a 'grand Ceremonial Overture' for the Moscow Exhibition of 1881. It came as easily to him as the Serenade for Strings, Op.48, he was composing at the same time, much to his own surprise, and he made no bones to Nadezhda von Meck as to which task pleased him more:

The overture will be very loud and noisy, but I wrote it without warmth or love so it will probably not have any artistic merit. But the Serenade, by contrast, I wrote from an inner compulsion; it is deeply felt and for that reason, I venture to think, is not without real merit.

The Overture, charting the triumph of the Russians (and the Russian winter) over Napoleon's invading army in 1812, is not as meretricious as Tchaikovsky made out. The final victory parade – bells, cannons, brass bands et al – is a shamelessly effective piece of bombast, but lower strings are imaginatively employed in the opening chant of the Orthodox hymn 'God Save the Russian people', and 'warmth and love' turn up

Tchaikovsky's manuscript for the opening bars of the 1812 Overture (Lebrecht)

in a memorable theme filched from a duet in *The Voyevoda*. Still, the *1812* Overture is not in the same league as the Serenade. Tchaikovsky's skill in making a melody out of a rising scale, or part of it, sustains the delightful Waltz and the ensuing Elégie; there is unforced ingenuity, too, in the linking of the Finale's Russian folksong with the flourish that begins the Serenade. It is a sunny, if not carefree, work, robust proof that Tchaikovsky was enjoying his summers as a free man.

His composure, and a new-found sense of security as his reputation at home and abroad seemed to be strengthening daily, were shattered early in 1881 when he learned that Nikolay Rubinstein had died in Paris on March 23. The loss of his own father the previous January had left him only with a feeling of peacefulness: 'I think these tears which I shed at the disappearance from this world of an upright man endowed with an angelic spirit had a beneficial effect on me. I feel enlightened and reconciled in spirit,' he told von Meck. The opposite was true of Rubinstein's death, following as it did close on the senseless assassination of Alexander II. At the funeral service in Paris he saw for the last time the face of the man who had fathered him through his early years in Moscow. 'He had altered beyond recognition ... I am terribly weighed down by grief.' He wrote to his patroness that he might yet become a true believer:

> *My mind is in confusion, and it could not be otherwise, a feeble intellect faced with such insoluble questions as* death, the aim and meaning of life, and its infinity or its finitude. *But the light of faith penetrates deeper and deeper into my soul.*

Yet it was because he had 'lost all interest in symphonic music' since Rubinstein's death, and not because he had turned to religion, that he began that summer on an *All-night Vigil*, Op.52, treating the melodies of the service as he fancied. It was a pendant to the *Liturgy of St John Chrysostom*, Op.41, which he had written three years earlier in an attempt to provide music in harmony with 'the Byzantine style of the architecture and the icons, with the whole structure of the Orthodox service'. Catherine the Great's court composer, Dmitry Bortnyansky, had failed in that respect, he thought, and his feelings were confirmed when, having completed the *All-night Vigil*, he turned to editing a collection of Bortnyansky's works. First-hand knowledge left him unimpressed. Bortnyansky was 'prolific mediocrity incarnate'; everything in his works was 'fluent, neat, pleasant, but monotonous and barren as a steppe'.

A true memorial to Rubinstein had to wait for the return of proper inspiration during his next Italian winter. He wanted to pay tribute again to Rubinstein's pianistic skills, and he took up the idea of solo strings and piano from the slow movement of the Second Concerto in a more conventional context, the piano trio. He knew it would please his patroness, too. Nadezhda von Meck had recently played host to a young pianist from Paris, Claude Debussy, who briefly joined forces for her private pleasure with her new house cellist and violinist, and she wanted Tchaikovsky to write something for them. Inevitably it pleased her, but it was not in the Meck household but at the Moscow Conservatoire exactly a year after Rubinstein's death that the Piano Trio, Op.50, received its first, private performance (Tchaikovsky had consulted the cellist, his friend Karl Albrecht, over the correct bow markings).

The unusual pattern follows that of Beethoven's last Piano Sonata – a dark first movement followed by a set of variations in brighter mood – though Tchaikovsky departs from his model by interrupting his serene second-movement remembrance of times past with the lament from the previous movement, dying away as a funeral march: a tribute undeniably from the heart.

In the last years of Alexander II's reign Tchaikovsky had begun to win influence in high places with the devoted, demanding friendship of the tsar's brother, the Grand Duke Konstantin Nikolayevich. He could only expect closer ties with the new ruler, Alexander III, duly acknowledged in the commissioning of a coronation cantata on the history of Moscow which he found far from laborious and a loan of 3,000 roubles to make life easier for his beloved servant Alexey, then undergoing the rigors of military service. The situation turned his roving operatic thoughts back to the Pushkin subject for which he had composed a single scene, *Poltava*, dealing with the machinations of Mazeppa, the Polish nobleman and would-be tyrant of the Ukraine, against Peter the Great. What had attracted Tchaikovsky at the beginning of 1882 was the love scene between the heroine Maria and Mazeppa, nothing more; but when he took up Viktor Burenin's libretto and realized that this would be another national-historical drama along the lines of *The Oprichnik*, he proceeded without much initial enthusiasm for the characters, though he seems as usual to have been in sympathy with his heroine and, as in *The Maid of Orléans*, the Finale – a bleak mad-scene for Maria as she cradles her dying true love Andrei – is most striking.

Otherwise, *Mazeppa* was hard work all the way; never before had a project given him so much trouble, he told his patroness. His attitude to opera had changed considerably after *Onegin*: it was 'a lower form of art than either symphonic or chamber music ... opera has the advantage of making it possible to influence the

Tsar Alexander III (AKG)

musical sensitivities of the *masses*, whereas the symphonic composer deals with a small and select public'. At least, with the new tsar's benevolent support, *Mazeppa* was lavishly staged in Moscow and St. Petersburg throughout the later part of February 1884, as handsome and well-rehearsed as the original production of *The Maid of Orléans* had been scenically threadbare and casually mounted. Times were indeed changing, and in October perfect preparation for a new *Eugene Onegin* in the Bolshoi and Maryinsky Theatre ensured that 'the masses' proclaimed Tchaikovsky's 'lyrical scenes' an authentic masterpiece. Modest was telling the truth when he wrote that this was the decisive point at which 'Pyotr Ilyich achieves the highest degree of popularity ever attained by a Russian composer within the borders of his native land'.

Kamenka no longer afforded the ideal retreat from the social pressures to which Tchaikovsky found himself increasingly persuaded to submit in the two capitals. When the whole family congregated there, it had never been quiet, but in the early

1880s it began to be fraught with tensions. First his sister fell prey to a nervous illness, and 'when she is ill the remaining members of the family are unhappy, such is the fanatical feeling of love and devotion that she inspires in them all'. Her mental problems were mirrored in the behavior of her eldest daughter Tanya. In the summer of 1882 Tchaikovsky found his once-vivacious niece 'poisoning herself with morphine, and poisoning her parents and everyone else living in her company with her attacks of illness, which are repeated daily because of the morphine. This unfortunate girl seems to live on earth solely in order to torment herself and others.' Now that Antonina, who had given birth to another man's child, no longer posed a threat, it must have seemed to Tchaikovsky that Tanya was his own special torment. First she flaunted her sexuality by parading before his ever-prudish eyes her passion for the new music teacher at Kamenka, Stanislav Blumenfeld. Then, at the end of the following January, she appeared in Tchaikovsky's Paris retreat – ostensibly sent abroad to be cured of her morphine addiction by the famous neurologist Charcot, but in fact pregnant by Blumenfeld. 'She is a person who inspires fear and dread in me ... the sight of her upsets and poisons every minute of one's life': such were his terrified reactions. But after the child, Georges-Léon, was born on May 8, and Tchaikovsky had made provisions for him to be taken in by a French family, he felt great tenderness towards the baby and 'a desire to be his protector'. His natural sympathy for Tanya, too, eventually got the better of his instinctive repulsion, though it was still difficult keeping the baby a secret from Sasha.

Georges-Léon, along with the baby daughter of Tchaikovsky's recently married brother Anatoly and the child of the Davydov's second daughter Vera, who had married a Rimsky-Korsakov distantly related to the composer, inspired a charming set of Children's Songs, Op.54 – including the famous 'Legend' often performed as a Christmas carol – as well as the delicately scored *Rêves d'enfant* movement of a new suite completed at Kamenka. In this Second Suite, Op.53, Tchaikovsky explored fresh possibilities in orchestral color, the most celebrated of which – if only because it makes this delightful work an expensive rarity in the concert hall – is a brief role for four accordions in the fantastical Scherzo burlesque. The Third Suite, Op.55, another pleasant task undertaken in the summer of 1884, achieved even greater fame during the composer's lifetime; its final Theme and Variations tend to be detached and played separately, though the first three movements are full of happy inspirations and include a *Valse mélancolique* every inch as singular as its famous successor in the *Pathétique* Symphony. Youthful promptings this time seem to have been less innocent; as one of only two surviving diaries reveals, Tchaikovsky was infatuated with his thirteen-year-old nephew Bob (Vladimir) Davydov, though he tried to keep his homosexual feelings under control.

It was time, all the same, to say a long-term farewell to Kamenka. He needed a home of his own, as he had realized when things were going badly with the Davydovs: 'I have no home anywhere, I can settle nowhere else in Russia, I am afraid of loneliness abroad; now I really am a sort of nomad and the thought weighs me down,' he told Modest. This nomadic existence allied him with romantic literature's most famous wanderer, Lord Byron's Manfred, and rekindled thoughts of a program on the subject which Balakirev had persuaded Stasov to outline to him back in the late 1860s; the inspiration then had been a performance of Berlioz's tribute to Byron, *Harold en Italie*, conducted by the composer. Balakirev had returned to take dramatic center stage in Tchaikovsky's life in 1882, and although Tchaikovsky had for a second time refused *Manfred*, on the grounds that Schumann's setting was sufficient, now in 1884 the seeds of his proposal bore autobiographical fruit. As with *Romeo and Juliet*, Balakirev's suggestions went further than an elaboration of Stasov's program to include a list of role models, including Tchaikovsky's own *Francesca da Rimini*, which does indeed lie behind the first movement. Wagner, amazingly enough, is a brooding presence here, too. Tchaikovsky had seen *Tristan und Isolde* for the first time in January 1883, and he maintained his verdict of old that the German composer's music-dramas were endless symphonies with the drama superimposed. Yet, again, the colors and harmonies must have impressed him, for the scholar David Brown draws a plausible link between the ominous music which brings the lovers face to face in *Tristan* and Tchaikovsky's striking initial presentation of Manfred's theme on low woodwind against the snap of lower strings. The first movement as a whole was the most imposing edifice Tchaikovsky had constructed since its counterpart in the Fourth Symphony. For his Scherzo and Andante he brought to perfection the varied orchestration he had been developing in the Suites; the *Manfred* Symphony falls flat only in the hero's unconvincing transfiguration at the end of the finale – exactly the kind of organ-crowned apotheosis that he had avoided in *The Maid of Orléans*. Though he later came, as usual, to doubt the value of what he had written, Tchaikovsky assessed his program symphony accurately at the time of the première: 'I myself think it's my best symphonic work, though because of its difficulty, impractibility and complexity it is doomed *to failure and to be ignored.*'

By the time he gave his fullest attention to the *Manfred* Symphony in April 1885, Tchaikovsky was a nomad no longer. On New Year's Day he had placed an advertisement in *The Police Gazette*: 'Single person seeks dacha/country estate to rent'.

The temporary outcome was a large house on the banks of the river at Maydanovo, 100 miles north of Moscow – pleasantly situated but tastelessly furnished, cold and falling into disrepair. It was a welcome enough retreat, though, for the revision of *Vakula the Smith*, and even in late winter nature delighted him. Nadezhda von Meck was always a sympathetic recipient of such effusions:

Frontispiece of the original score for The Maid of Orléans *(Lebrecht)*

I love our Russian countryside more than any other, and for me the Russian landscape in winter has an incomparable charm. This, incidentally, in no way stops me loving both Switzerland and Italy, but somehow differently. I find it particularly difficult to agree today that the Russian countryside is unattractive. It's a marvellous day, sunny, the snow is glistening like myriads of diamonds and is thawing slightly, my window gives me a wide view right into the distance. It's wonderful and spacious, you can breathe properly in these immense horizons.

By the summer, when Tchaikovsky had still found no alternative residence, there were drawbacks: 'fine grounds, pretty views, marvellous bathing – but it's all ruined by the people coming to their dachas for their holidays'. His routine, observed only by his pet dog and the ever-faithful Alexey, was later outlined by Modest: early rising, total privacy for creation between 9:30 and midday, a two-hour walk after lunch which gave rise to musical ideas, work from five to seven and another walk before supper. The evening was given over to guests, never to composition, and at eleven he went to his room to read and write his diary before going to sleep. Modest makes only one crucial omission: when depressed, his brother would drink himself into oblivion.

The 'depressing' subject of *Manfred* certainly made him melancholy, until enthusiasm took over and he worked exhaustively for four months. In the autumn, he moved to a smaller, quieter house on the same estate and began a new opera, *The Enchantress*. Like *The Maid of Orléans* and *Mazeppa*, this was to be 'music for the masses', as he made quite clear to his patroness when he lamented that *Manfred* 'will be played once or twice and will then vanish for ever … whereas opera, and in fact

The Queen of Spades: *The scene in the countess's bedchamber designed by Richard Hudson for Glyndebourne, 1992 (Catherine Ashmore)*

only opera, draws you closer to people, gives the real public some affinity with your music …' Quite why he settled on Ippolit Shpazhinsky's ramshackle melodrama remains a mystery, even if he did claim for the heroine a different kind of potential than his playwright had seen. 'There is a *moral power and a beauty* buried at the

Evetkova as Kuma in The Enchantress, *1900*
(Lebrecht)

bottom of this loose woman's heart' he wrote, mentioning Goethe's 'eternal womanhood' and thinking, surely, of Bizet's Carmen. For Kuma, the enchantress and enslaver of men whose misfortune it is to be the mistress of a prince and, ultimately, the lover of his son, needs the wide, open spaces of the Volga just as Carmen needs the liberty of the Andalusian mountains. Unfortunately, she has none of that lady's musical sensuality, though Tchaikovsky tried to put his heart and soul into what he called 'the *most important* scene of the opera' where Kuma and Yury, the young prince, fall in love. The light-hearted first act has plenty of Russian folksiness but little of *Vakula*'s freshness, though the tragic fourth act can be effective; Tchaikovsky's lugubrious scoring for woodwind was to find a home in his next, and last, opera *The Queen of Spades*.

Work on *The Enchantress* took much longer than he had envisaged, and it was not completed until the middle of May 1887.

Then he embarked on a second journey to an outpost of the Russian empire, Tiflis (Tbilisi) in Georgia, where his brother Anatoly was public prosecutor, and there he composed his only other large-scale work of the year, a Fourth Suite which he (unwillingly) titled *Mozartiana*. It was a tribute in the centenary year of *Don Giovanni* to the composer he still revered above all others – even above Beethoven, whom he saw as the awe-inspiring Michelangelo of music, while Mozart was Raphael, human and much more loveable.

The four movements of the suite were generally tasteful orchestrations of piano pieces (the third being the now-famous motet 'Ave verum corpus' based on a piano transcription by Liszt, which may explain why it sounds syrupy to our ears), and Tchaikovsky explained his motives in a preface to the score: 'The author had in mind to provide a new occasion for the more frequent performances of these pearls of musical art, unpretentious in form, but filled with unrivalled beauties.'

The first visit to Tiflis the previous year had been notable for three things: a relationship with a local army officer, whose suicide shortly after Tchaikovsky's departure distressed him beyond measure; the championship of his music there, especially a new production of *Mazeppa*, by a young composer and conductor newly graduated from the St. Petersburg Conservatoire, Ippolitov-Ivanov; and his first glimpse of the East. He conveyed his delight in 'a situation utterly new' to Modest:

The streets are unusually narrow, as in Venice; downstairs on both sides is an endless row of small shops and craft establishments of all sorts where the locals sit cross-legged working in view of the passers-by. There are bakers and special kinds of food shops where they bake and fry various things. It's very interesting and novel.

He continued to savor the exotic on his travels after this happiest of months in Tbilisi, cruising along the Turkish coast of the Black Sea to Constantinople, then on to Greece and the south coast of Italy before the ship docked in Marseilles. In Paris his task was to tie up the process of Georges-Léon's adoption by his eldest brother Nikolay and his wife Olga, and to take him back to Russia. There was a terrible sequel to this: at the end of January 1887, Tanya collapsed and died at a masked ball. 'Poor Tanya!' he wrote to Anatoly's wife Parasha. 'Now that all's finished, you involuntarily forget all her dark sides, and remember only what a marvellous girl she was twelve years ago.' In the meantime, Antonina had recommenced her letter-writing offensive. Tchaikovsky obliged her demands for money with a very generous allowance, later increased by a gift from the tsar, but a meeting was more out of the question than ever before. He told Modest:

> ... *she informed me that she had three children, all in a foundling hospital, one of them apparently called Pyotr after me, and suggested that I should bring up one or all of them. In addition she sent me an embroidered shirt and asked me to dedicate something to her. She really and truly has gone mad.*

Indeed she had. Antonina outlived Tchaikovsky by twenty-five years, but she spent most of them in a lunatic asylum.

In public life, Tchaikovsky continued to use his new-found fame and prosperity to help others. A rare excursion into social welfare was his provision, and continued support, of a school in Maidanovo for the underprivileged children of local parents. As a Moscow director of the Russian Musical Society, he became a more enlightened

Sergei Taneyev (Lebrecht)

kind of Balakirev figure to a new generation of younger composers, including the talented Arensky, and he acted in everyone's best interests when he engineered the appointment of the twenty-nine-year-old Taneyev as Director of the Moscow Conservatoire. Although he still needed his country retreat – he had recently moved to another house in the Klin district – he could face official duties with far more confidence than before. At the end of 1886, he once more took up the conductor's baton he had wielded only three times before in his life – disastrously in 1865 and 1868, more successfully conducting the *Marche Slave* in 1877. He had decided to conduct the first performance of the revised *Vakula, Cherevichki* (*The Slippers*), and astonished orchestral players at the rehearsals by overcoming his shame and embarrassment with a remarkable show of confidence. The assessment he made to Nadezhda von Meck early in January 1887 marked the beginning of a new era:

Of course conducting does not come easily to me and demands a great effort from my nervous system. But I cannot deny that it also gives me great delight. First, I have the pleasure of realizing that I have overcome my innate and unhealthy shyness; secondly, it is remarkably pleasant for the composer of a new opera to be able himself to guide the course of his composition and not to have continually to approach the conductor, asking him to correct this or that mistake; thirdly, at every stage I see such genuine signs of support for me on the part of the performers that I am deeply touched and moved.

The première proved highly successful; so, too, did Tchaikovsky's return to conducting his own orchestral works two months later. 'Even if my attempts at conducting have cost me an immense and difficult struggle with myself, if they have taken several years off my life, I have no regrets,' he told his patroness after this performance. The first performance of *The Enchantress* in October turned out to be a fiasco, though not from a conducting point of view, and there was rich compensation to hand: Tchaikovsky's reputation as a conductor had spread to Western Europe, and he embarked on the first of two three-month tours at the beginning of 1888. So the set pattern of his life changed for the third time in the years following the crisis of his marriage.

'Do you recognize in this musician travelling round Europe the same man who only a few months ago hid from social life and lived in solitude, whether abroad or in the country?!!' he asked Mrs. von Meck. Homesickness plagued him, but 'artistic vanity' invariably gained the upper hand. He launched his series of programs, or half-programs, featuring his own music in Leipzig, following in the hallowed footsteps of Schumann and Mendelssohn who had both conducted in the

Original program for the first concert Tchaikovsky conducted in Western Europe, at Leipzig in 1888 (Lebrecht)

Zwölftes

ABONNEMENT-CONCERT

im Saale des

Neuen Gewandhauses zu Leipzig

Donnerstag, den 5. Januar 1888.

ERSTER THEIL.

Suite für Orchester (Op. 43) von PETER TSCHAIKOWSKY. (Zum ersten Male. Unter Leitung des Componisten.)
I. Introduzione e Fuga. — II. Divertimento. — III. Intermezzo. — IV. Marche miniature. — V. Gavotte.

ZWEITER THEIL.

Concert für Pianoforte (G dur) von LUDWIG VAN BEETHOVEN, vorgetragen von Fräulein *Fanny Davies* aus London.
I. Allegro moderato. — II. Andante con moto. — III. Rondo.

Gewandhaus, then on to Hamburg and Berlin – where *Francesca da Rimini* was suppressed (in 1888, but not on his next year's visit). He could not have anticipated the reception in Prague, which was bound up with anti-German, pro-Slav feelings: 'They received me as though I were the representative not just of Russian music but of all of Russia.' When he ended his thanksgiving speech (in Czech) by saying that 'The days I have passed here are quite the best and happiest of my entire life', he meant it. Paris, where he conducted two half-concerts, welcomed him as a Russian, too, but that was more dictated by prevailing fashions. A London appearance secured his future fame in England, and the return visit in 1889 reintroduced him to the fog-enveloped city he knew so well from reading his beloved Dickens' *Bleak House*. At the end of both tours he traveled on to Tiflis, fatigued but unable to conceal a deep-seated spirit of delight.

Even in earlier trips to Paris he had never met so many other composers on his travels. He had two years in which to become accustomed to the sympathetic, straightforward personality of Brahms, though he was to retain his reservations about Brahms's music, in which he continued to find 'something dry, cold that alienates my heart … His *depth* is not real … His is an empty chasm'. He was not lacking in perception when he found little out of the ordinary in the F minor Symphony of the twenty-three-year-old Richard Strauss, whom he met in Berlin; Strauss's true originality was yet to flourish. He admired Dvořák's sincerity and warmth both as a man and as a composer. But it was with Edward Grieg that he formed the closest ties, finding in his 'deeply human' and very Norwegian inspirations a kinship with the Russian soul. Back in Russia, he dedicated to Grieg the first of two orchestral works, the darkly scored fantasia *Hamlet*, Op.67a, which soon evolved into a portrait of his own darker side along *Manfred* lines (the openings of symphony and overture have much in common).

The more important project, a Fifth Symphony, has a less familiar dedicatee, the arch-conservative Hamburg teacher Theodor Avé-Lallement. Tchaikovsky seems to have accepted his advice in Hamburg – to settle in Germany and absorb 'proper' classical traditions – without rancor, and in one respect he did follow it in his Fifth Symphony, Op.64, by omitting the ubiquitous cymbals; although the final victory parade, a rather hollow triumph over fate, is exactly the kind of brashly scored passage which made the old German master shudder. In the Fifth's otherwise perfect proportions and the careful handling of the motto theme, a

Johannes Brahms (Mansell)

tribute to Glinka heard at the very beginning of the symphony on low-lying clarinets, Tchaikovsky did however follow western guidelines. Even so, there was an underlying program outlined in Tchaikovsky's private notes:

> *Intr. Total submissions before Fate – or, what is the same thing, the inscrutable design of Providence.*
> *Allegro. 1. Murmurs, doubts, laments, reproaches against ... XXX.*
> *2. Shall I cast myself into the embraces of* faith?

If XXX is the composer's homosexuality, then the famous Andante cantabile is an open-hearted confession of love – object unknown – with few of the poignant twists that had marked previous themes along the same lines. It is plausible that the horn melody should have been matched to the words 'O, que je t'aime! O mon amie!'; whatever the inspiration, Tchaikovsky never wrote a finer slow movement, though to his patroness he rated the Fifth as a whole lower than its predecessor, '*our* symphony'.

His next task was a delightful one, and a chance to see the inadequate circumstances which had beset *Swan Lake* redeemed. In 1881, four years after that disastrous première, Ivan Vsevolozhsky had been appointed Director of the Imperial Theatres. He was a persuasive advocate of improved standards through better funding – Tchaikovsky's *Mazeppa* had done well by him – but also a man of vision. He provided what we might now call the 'book' of a new ballet for which he wanted Tchaikovsky to write the music – an adaptation of the French fairytale *La belle au bois dormant* by Charles Perrault, known to us as *The Sleeping Beauty*. 'I want to stage it in the style of Louis XIV, allowing the musical fantasy to run high and melodies to be written in the spirit of Lully, Bach, Rameau and such-like,' he told Tchaikovsky in May 1888. 'In the last act there needs to be a quadrille made from all of Perrault's fairy-stories – Puss in Boots, Tom Thumb, Cinderella, Bluebeard and such like.' His composer was 'thrilled beyond words' by the completed scenario when he received it that August; all he now needed was a meeting with Vsevolozhsky and the choreographer Marius Petipa, also a man of genius, which took place in November – though his impatience led him to sketch the greater part of the Prologue a month earlier.

He provided the details of his progress, mostly undertaken at his new country home in the woods at Frolovskoye, in his diary: 'I finished the sketches on June 7, 1889 at 8 p.m. Praise be to God! In all I worked ten days in October, three weeks in January, and now a week, so, in all, about forty days.' The scoring took longer, and little wonder: the endless ingenuity of his writing for woodwind, solo and collective, in the miniature set pieces for the fairies at Princess Aurora's christening and the fairytale characters at her wedding 120 years later remains one of his greatest achievements. The ballet music also operates on a deeper level: Tchaikovsky owed more than he realized to Wagner in the subtle transformations at work in the long-term battle between good and evil of the Lilac Fairy and Carabosse, though he stamped both themes with his own experience. There are inevitable reminders, too, of another powerful myth, that of Brünnhilde asleep on the rock in *The Ring*, which help to enrich the most remarkable symphonic stretch of the score as the prince makes his way through the forest to the enchanted palace and violins sustain the note of C for exactly one hundred bars of music. Tchaikovsky's sense of enchantment and his ceremonial music in the French and Russian imperial styles were lavishly served by Vsevolozhsky and Petipa at the first performance, though its success was pre-empted by disappointment at the dress rehearsal on January 14, 1890, as the composer's diary reveals: 'Rehearsal of the ballet attended by the *Tsar*. "Very nice"!!!!! His majesty was very haughty with me. Pity about him.'

Crowd fatigue did not prevent Tchaikovsky from starting work on his next offering for the Vsevolozhsky regime almost immediately; since he would be composing in the environment of his beloved Florence, a change would be as good as a rest. His choice of operatic subject had moved very close to Chekhov in October 1889, when the man Tchaikovsky described to Modest as 'our great new Russian literary talent' set the seal on their friendship by dedicating a collection of short stories to his musical hero. He also sent him a further book of stories with the inscription 'To Pyotr Ilyich Tchaikovsky, from his future librettist', though frustratingly we know no more about this. In any case, Tchaikovsky's thoughts turned back shortly afterwards to one of two projected Pushkin adaptations, an opera on *The Queen of Spades*, for which Modest – a playwright whose original efforts his brother had long tried to champion, usually in vain – had already written a libretto (intended for another composer). The nature of the tale turned his Italian winter holiday into something of a nightmare: by the middle of February he had reached the scene in Pushkin's narrative where the gloomy Teutonic hero Hermann, desperate to know the secret of three cards possessed by an old, mysterious countess, enters her bedchamber and frightens her to death. 'My work has made me very nervous. It's funny, but even my inspiration drives me crazy and creates difficulties', he wrote in his diary, and nearing completion in March, he told Modest, 'Unless I

Sleeping Beauty: *The Rose Adagio at Covent Garden, 1986 (Catherine Ashmore)*

am making some dreadful and unforgivable mistake ... in Scene Four ... I experience such a sense of fear, dread and shock that the audience too is *bound* to feel the same, at least in some degree.'

The Countess-Hermann scene is certainly the most forward-looking piece of music-theater Tchaikovsky ever wrote, moving with a frightening intensity from the nervous, shadowy prelude through a hobgoblinish chorus of ladies-in-waiting to a remarkable monologue for the Countess as she reflects on bygone days and then to her wordless terror as Hermann accosts her. It influenced the swift-moving operas of Janáček, among others, who wrote admiringly of this 'music of horror' in 1896 and paid tribute to it in his first operatic masterpiece *Jenůfa*. And yet elsewhere in *The Queen of Spades* there is much that is conventional grand opera, that holds up the macabre action and defuses the spare narrative of Pushkin's story. In place of the author's ironical observation of Hermann's decline into lunacy, Tchaikovsky ends up identifying with his obsessive hero, has him blow his brains out and makes his heroine, Lisa, commit suicide by jumping into St. Petersburg's Winter Canal (in Pushkin she lives on to marry a nice young man). There are splendid homages to Catherine the Great, Mozartian pastorals and cheery Russian drinking songs: all good music, but not good drama. The spectacle of the St. Petersburg first night, on December 19, 1890, scored a predictable triumph, though, and for once Tchaikovsky had a singer to play the protagonist whom he admired and had in mind from the start, the tenor Nikolay Figner, whose wife Medea played opposite him as Lisa.

Between the swift completion of the opera in June and the première, Tchaikovsky honored his long-standing membership of the St. Petersburg Chamber Music Society with a string sextet, *Souvenir de Florence*, Op.70, a sunny throwback to his liking for classical forms, with the occasional ghost from *The Queen of Spades* flitting across the canvas; his main worry was that he was 'writing for the orchestra and just rearranging … for six string instruments', and he revised it the following year. He also composed another *Voyevoda*, Op.78, no relation to the subject of his first opera but an orchestral tone poem on the Pushkin poem in which a jealous official orders his servant to shoot his adulterous wife but is himself killed; his swift death is a prototype for the autobiographical demise in the Finale of the

Maria Slavin as the ancient, mysterious countess in
The Queen of Spades, *1891 première (Lebrecht)*

Pathétique Symphony. *The Voyevoda* is a short but effectively lugubrious piece which Tchaikovsky was wrong to wish destroyed, and there may well be autobiography here, too; for at the time of composition in Tiflis he was stunned by the news that Nadezhda von Meck had terminated their written relationship. The reason given was that she faced financial ruin and could no longer support him – it was wounding enough to Tchaikovsky to think that she thought of money as the only reason for their friendship – but when it turned out that her finances were more or less restored, and she refused to rekindle the correspondence, he was shattered. He wrote to their intermediary, her son-in-law Pachulski:

> *Perhaps it is because I never knew N.F.* personally *that she seemed to me to be the ideal of a human being; I could not have imagined inconstancy in such a demigoddess; I would have thought that the world would fall apart before N.F. would change in her attitude to me. But this is what has happened and it turns upside down my view of people and my faith in the best of them; it disturbs my peace of mind and ruins that portion of happiness which fate has allotted to me.*

The wounds never healed, unless we are to believe the account of Nadezhda's granddaughter Galina von Meck, who claims that Tchaikovsky, weeks before his own death, asked her mother to send on his plea for mutual forgiveness, a request that was apparently granted. Why the rift occurred – whether Mrs. von Meck discovered and disapproved of her beloved friend's homosexuality, whether she feared his discovery of her own affair long past, or whether her jealous children brought pressure to bear – remains an enigma.

The Nutcracker: *the battle of the Nutcracker and the Mouse-King in the Royal Ballet production (Zoë Dominic)*

Another sudden parting soon followed: on March 28, 1891 Sasha died, poisoned by her addiction to alcohol, morphine and other drugs. Though Modest tried to prevent it, news reached Tchaikovsky in Rouen on the eve of his most important expedition yet, a conducting tour of America. He resolved to continue, sailing over the ocean with the feeling 'that I am not myself but somebody else ... Sasha's death, with all its painful associations, is like a recollection from some very remote past

Tchaikovsky and his brothers in 1890. From left to right: Anatol, Nikolay, Ippolit, Pyotr and Modest (Lebrecht)

which I can drive away without any particular difficulty, and then once more I think of the passing interests of that creature who is not *me*, but who is travelling to America *inside me*'. He was soon diverted by seasickness and the company of some disreputable but entertaining second-class passengers. Once in New York, despite the usual homesickness, he warmed to American life. He liked being 'a much bigger fish here than in Europe'; he enjoyed the colossal dimensions of the buildings, and admired the profiteering Americans' attitude to art, exemplified by the brand new Music (soon to be Carnegie) Hall whose opening he had been invited to celebrate. He traveled to Niagara Falls – 'difficult to express in words' – and conducted his own music in Baltimore and Philadelphia as well as New York. He was, above all, very impressed by the archetypal self-made man, Scots-born Andrew Carnegie:

> ... *an amazing eccentric, who from being a telegraph boy, was transformed with the passing of the years into one of America's richest men but who has remained a simple, modest man who does not at all turn up his nose at anyone, inspires an unusual warmth of feeling in me, perhaps because he is overflowing with goodwill towards me ... He grasped me by the hand, crying out that I was uncrowned, but the most genuine king of music, embraced me (without kissing; here men never kiss each other) and in describing my greatness, stood on tiptoe and raised his arms above his head, and finally delighted the whole company by imitating me conducting.*

Such friendships, and the triumph of learning to communicate fully in English, renewed Tchaikovsky's confidence, and he arrived back in Russia at the end of May in high spirits.

His return to Frolovskoye was not a happy one: the woods in which he loved to walk had been destroyed. So he moved back to Maidanovo and resumed the task which he had begun before his American tour – work on a Vsevolozhsky commission, a double-bill of a one-act opera and a two-act ballet. The ballet was a very free adaptation of *The Nutcracker and the Mouse-King* by the fantastical German romantic writer E.T.A. Hoffmann, and he wanted to complete it quickly so as to move on to the opera. At Maidanovo he sketched the second act, excited by the prospect of including in it a part for the new musical instrument he had discovered in Paris, 'something half-way between a small piano and a Glockenspiel, with a marvellous, heavenly sound'. It crept into musical history with a supporting role in *The Voyevoda*, but it was as the Sugar Plum Fairy's personal property in *The Nutcracker* that the celesta (or the Celesta Mustel, as its inventor patented it) first achieved immortality. Tchaikovsky's attitude to composition was characteristically capricious. 'Writing the ballet has cost me an effort because I could feel a decline in my powers of invention,' he wrote to Taneyev after completing the sketches in early July, but soon he was newly embarked on the opera and confided to Modest: 'Now I think the ballet is good and the opera is nothing special.' Then composition took a turn for the better: 'I know now that *Yolanta* will not disgrace itself.'

Posterity has decided in favor of *The Nutcracker* – at least in the West, though in Russia *Yolanta*, Op.69, has had some success. The subject matter of Henrick Hertz's play *King René's Daughter*, from which Modest drew the libretto for his brother's opera, may seem untenable to modern-day sensibilities. Blind Yolanta lives in a world of gentle, *Nutcracker*-like enchantments, ignorant of her sightlessness and curable only through the will to love and truly live – an offensive notion unless you

A scene from the first act of the Royal Ballet Nutcracker *(Zoë Dominic)*

take the blindness merely as a symbol of the sheltered life. Tchaikovsky was more interested in the pathos of his heroine's situation, and musically she comes close to the sufferings of the teenage Tatyana in *Eugene Onegin*. The other principal characters are mere ciphers, though they all have attractive, sometimes inspired, arias to sing, and the duet in which the gallant tenor hero, Vaudemont, awakens Yolanta's curiosity is the heart and soul of this static, short (hour-and-a-half) drama – even if Tchaikovsky did see fit to plunder one of his old teacher Anton Rubinstein's better melodies. The plagiarism did not pass unnoticed on the first night, December 18, 1892, though again Tchaikovsky had the best advocates for his hero and heroine in Nikolay and Medea Figner.

The sweet-toothed scenario of the ballet offered another opportunity for a Vsevolozhsky spectacular, though Tchaikovsky noted it was all too much – 'The eye tires of so much opulence.' The ear, however, does not, because Tchaikovsky had excelled himself in the ingenuity and variety of his orchestration. As well as the numbers of the divertissement, which make up the greater part of the famous Concert Suite Tchaikovsky extracted for preview in 1891, there is genius in the use of simple musical means to conjure the great transformation scenes of Act One, their ascending melodies echoed by the descending scales of the Pas de Deux in Act Two. Flimsy the action may be, but the composer made sure that each act was well shaped. If *The Sleeping Beauty*, Op.66, a much longer score, is more generous with its inspirations, *The Nutcracker* is Tchaikovsky's most perfect ballet.

Tchaikovsky's years of fame had settled into an inevitable routine: concert tours abroad in the winter (and he was now conducting other composers' music as well as his own), the greater part of his compositional work done at whichever country home

Alexander Glazunov: portrait by
Repin 1887 (AKG)

above: *Tchaikovsky's last home at Klin (David Nice)*

opposite: *Tchaikovsky's memorial ouside the Moscow Conservatory (David Nice)*

ВЕЛИКОМУ РУССКОМУ
КОМПОЗИТ · РУ
ПЕТРУ ИЛЬИЧУ
ЧАЙКОВСКОМУ

he happened to be renting, and finally the usual round of family visits and public engagements. He continued to support the younger generation – especially Taneyev and Alexander Glazunov – by championing and conducting their music. Two geniuses in the making caught his attention. He noted the 'astounding' talent of Hamburg's conductor-in-residence, Gustav Mahler, and admired two works by the nineteen-year-old Sergei Rachmaninov – the 'delightful' opera *Aleko* and the celebrated C# minor Prelude.

Occasionally the pattern was broken, notably by a week of self-inflicted 'rest-cure' boredom in detested Vichy with his beloved nephew Bob (who did not reciprocate his intense affections) in June 1892 and a trip to Cambridge the following June to receive an honorary doctorate. He conducted two works which meant more to him than the usual repertoire shored up for foreign tours – his Fourth Symphony in London, in a concert shared with his future fellow graduate Saint-Saëns (inevitably overshadowed), and *Francesca da Rimini* for the Cambridge University Musical Society. He found Saint-Saëns and the Italian composer Boito good companions at the graduation ceremony, loathed Max Bruch and dealt as best he could with the bizarre ritual, which included, by tradition, whistling, hooting and singing from the students while the Latin speeches of honor were recited. The impression he made as a person was best summed up by the conductor Alexander Mackenzie: 'His unaffected modesty, kindly manner and real gratitude for any trifling service rendered contributed to the favourable impression made by a lovable man.'

As usual, he enjoyed the rigors of his expedition most in retrospect. It had been a pleasant diversion, one he had nearly decided not to take, if only so as not to interrupt the unprecedented flow of inspiration which had taken hold of his work in

Tchaikovsky receiving his honorary doctorate at Cambridge, May 1893 (Lebrecht)

his new (and, as it turned out, last) home in Klin. A set of piano pieces, Op.72, dashed off to rectify the 'disgusting condition' of his financial affairs and mostly in the charming, salon-miniature vein which had been his most distinguished contribution to solo piano music and six fine songs, Op.73, were overshadowed by the need to score a new orchestral work. It was a fresh start, similar in outline to the 'symphony with a secret programme' he had begun in 1892 but abandoned (ideas were subsequently reworked for a one-movement Third Piano Concerto, which proves the themes to be undistinguished). He wrote about his 'present happy frame of mind' over the new symphony to Bob, its eventual dedicatee, early in 1893:

Whilst I was on my travels I had an idea for another symphony, a programme symphony this time; but the programme will be left as an enigma – let people guess it for themselves – and the symphony will actually be called 'Programme Symphony' (No. 6). This programme is so intensely personal that as I was mentally composing it on my travels I frequently wept copiously. When I got back I settled to the sketches and I worked with such fervour and speed that in less than four days I had completely finished the first movement ... From the point of view of form there will be much that is new in this symphony, and the Finale, incidentally, will not be a noisy Allegro, but, on the contrary, a very unhurried Adagio. How glorious it is to realize that my time is not yet over and that I can still work.

There had indeed been nothing like the dark, tragic and controlled Adagio lamentoso in the history of the symphony, and if there were to be further examples of slow movements serving as finales in the symphonies of Mahler, then they were

Klin: Tchaikovsky's piano, on which winners of the Tchaikovsky Competition have given celebratory recitals (AKG)

Sketches for the second movement of the Sixth Symphony Pathétique *(AKG)* inspired by Tchaikovsky's example. In his long first movement he created a development more shattering even than the doom-laden Coda to Manfred's wanderings in the mountains, at the same time keeping a firm grip on his vast symphonic structure; the middle movements, a Waltz in the unusual, gracious meter of 5/4 and a March-Scherzo, first brilliantly then brazenly orchestrated, served their purpose in the scheme of things.

How far was this tragic drama a reflection of Tchaikovsky's state of mind at the time? There can be no doubt that in this, '*by far the most sincere* of all my pieces', he had bared his torment over the forced concealment of his sexual nature and relived the crisis of his marriage in 1877. Since then, though, he had never considered suicide, and while his moods continued to fluctuate dramatically, he was slowly achieving a new piece of mind. Certainly the finished symphony made him proud, pleased and happy. He had found some consolation for his way of life in the writings of Spinoza, who equated God with nature and stressed that condemnation of a man's desires came from society and not from a higher power. What depressed him in summer 1893 was the number of close friends dead or dying – his colleague from Moscow Conservatoire days Karl Albrecht, the Shilovsky brothers and the poet Apukhtin. He turned down the Grand Duke Konstantin's suggestion of a *Requiem* to verses by Apukhtin because 'my most recent symphony … is imbued with a spirit very close to that which also infuses the *Requiem*'. He conducted the first performance in St. Petersburg on October 28, to a subdued audience – 'it's not that the people don't like it, but they are somewhat puzzled by it' – and it was Modest who immediately came up with the title *Pathétique* (*Pateticheskaya*). Nine days later, Tchaikovsky was dead.

Modest's version of this unprecedented end was the one most commonly accepted until recently. According to him, on November 2 Tchaikovsky drank a glass of unboiled water at lunch in the flat they shared, and contracted cholera. So anxious was Modest 'to dispel all the conflicting rumours' that he published a lengthy account of the circumstances a week after his brother's death. Unfortunately, his version did not tally in its details with the report of the only other man in a position to substantiate death from cholera, Tchaikovsky's doctor Lev Bertenson. Suspicions were already aroused. The fair-minded Rimsky-Korsakov found it very strange indeed that the body of a cholera victim should be laid out for people to pay their respects, and stranger still that he saw one of Tchaikovsky's friends kiss the head and face; he was not afraid to say so in his memoirs. In her search for the truth Alexandra Orlova, the former archivist of the Tchaikovsky home and museum at Klin, consulted a professor and a doctor of tropical medicine and found that at least four of the facts in the accounts did not tally with what we know of cholera.

So it had to be suicide. But what would drive Tchaikovsky, who as we have seen had no thoughts at any time earlier in 1893 of ending his life, to that extreme? Orlova provided the answer, on the evidence of at least one person who seems to have told the truth. This was Elizaveta Jacobi, wife of one of Tchaikovsky's former fellow students at the School of Jurisprudence. Nikolay Jacobi, Deputy Chief Procurator for the Department of Criminal Appeal in the Senate, had been handed a letter to the tsar from one Count Stenbock-Fermor who, outraged at the composer's attentiveness to his nephew, threatened to expose his homosexuality. According to his wife, Jacobi convened a 'court of honour' comprising eight former students of the School of Jurisprudence, which decided that to save his and the School's honor, Tchaikovsky

Portrait of Tchaikovsky in the last year of his life by Kuznetsov (AKG)

should take his own life. He promised, took poison and died several days later.

Alexander III – many of whose courtiers were known to be homosexual, and who might have turned a blind eye to the scandal – ordered a state funeral, with honors: for the first time, a common citizen was given a memorial service in Kazan Cathedral (8,000 mourners were admitted, though 60,000 had applied for a ticket) and the ensuing procession down the Nevsky Prospect came to an end at the Alexander Nevsky cemetery, where Tchaikovsky was given a splendid tomb crowned by angels alongside the graves of Glinka and Borodin.

Just over a week later, the faithful Napravnik conducted a second performance of the *Pathétique* Symphony in St. Petersburg, putting the seal on the romantic legend that Tchaikovsky had prophesied his own death in his greatest symphony. Among a grateful future generation of composers, Stravinsky would acknowledge his gift for life-enhancing melody, proclaiming *The Sleeping Beauty* his best work, and it was his friend and critic Laroche who pre-empted his own eloquent tribute to the kindest of men with wise words at the time of that ballet's première:

An elegist by nature, inclined to melancholy, and even to a certain despair, he has shown in those kinds of composition officially labelled 'serious' a seriousness of another kind, a seriousness of thought, a frequent sadness and melancholy, not infrequently a nagging feeling of spiritual pain, and this, if one may so express it, minor part of his being … has been more grasped and esteemed. But alongside this there is another Tchaikovsky: nice, happy, brimming with health, inclined to humour.

This was as true of the person as it was of the composer. He knew probably more joy than sorrow in the last few years of his life, and so much of his music expresses that feeling of being, at last, at one with the world. His death, then, was not the tragedy of an overwrought neurotic, but the tragedy of a healthily creative genius who, had he lived, could not have gone on to write another *Pathétique* – that vein was surely exhausted – but would certainly have created more gentle, happy music.

Tchaikovsky on his deathbed (Lebrecht)

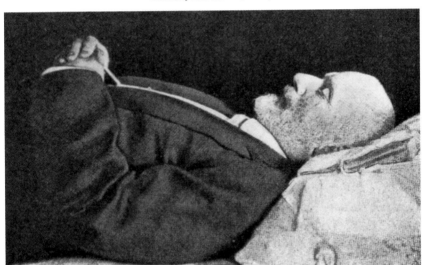

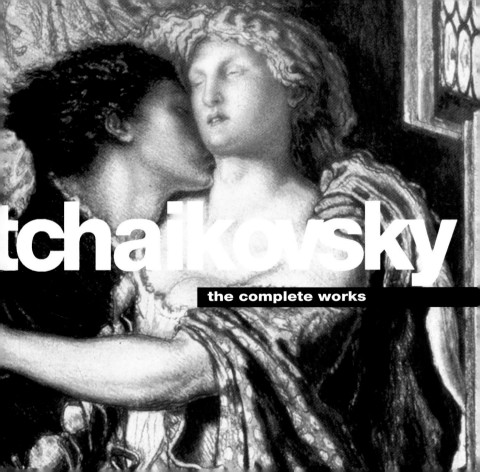

tchaikovsky

the complete works

Most of Tchaikovsky's works are cataloged according to Opus (work) numbers. The following list is ordered, where possible, according to the dates of the works.

Anastasie Valse for piano (1854)

'My genius, my angel, my friend': song (Fet) (1857–60)

'Song of Zemfira' (Pushkin) (1857–60)

'Who goes…': song (Apukhtin) (1857–60)

'Mezzanotte': song (in Italian – author unknown) (1860–1)

Allegro in F minor for piano (incomplete) (1863–4)

Theme and Variations in A minor for piano (1863–4)

'At bedtime' for unaccompanied chorus (Ogaryov) (1863–4)

The Storm: overture to Ostrovsky's play, Op. 76 (1864)

String Quartet movement in B♭ (1865)

Piano Sonata in C# minor, Op. 80 (1865)

Characteristic Dances, Op. 76 (1865 – revised as
Dances of the Hay Maidens in *The Voyevoda*, 1868)

Overture in F major for small orchestra
(1865, revised for large orchestra in 1866)

'An die Freude': cantata (Schiller/Aksakov) (1865)

Concert Overture in C minor (1866)

Symphony No. 1 in G minor, Op. 13, *Winter Daydreams*
(1866, revised 1874)

Festival Overture on the Danish National Anthem, Op. 15 (1866)

Two Pieces for piano, Op. 1: *Scherzo à la Russe* (1867);
Impromptu (1863–4)

Introduction and Mazurka for Ostrovsky's
Dmitriy the Pretender and Vassily Shuisky (1867)

Souvenir de Hapsal for piano, Op. 2: *Scherzo*; *Chant sans paroles* (1867)

Fatum: symphonic poem, Op. 77 (1868)

The Voyevoda: opera in three acts, Op. 3
(Ostrovsky/Tchaikovsky) (1867–8)

Valse caprice for piano, Op. 4 (1868)

Undine: opera in three acts – only several fragments survive
(de la Motte Fouqué/Sollogub) (1869)

Romeo and Juliet: Fantasy Overture (1869, revised 1870 and 1880)

Six Romances, Op. 6 (1869) :
'Do not believe, my friend' (A. Tolstoy);
'Not a word, O my friend' (Hartmann/Plescheyev);
'Both bitter and sweet' (Rostopchina);
'A tear trembles' (A. Tolstoy);
'Why?' (Heine/Mey);
'None but the lonely heart' (Goethe/Mey)

'Chorus of flowers and insects' for a projected opera,
Mandragora (Rachinsky) (1869–70)

Capriccio for piano, Op. 8 (1870)

Three Pieces for piano, Op. 9: *Reverie*; *Polka de Salon*;
Mazurka de Salon (1870)

'To forget so soon': song (Apukhtin) (1870)

'Nature and love': trio for two sopranos, contralto and piano
(Tchaikovsky) (1870)

String Quartet No. 1 in D, Op. 11 (1871; Andante cantabile later
scored for cello and orchestra, also performed by full string orchestra
with Tchaikovsky's approval)

The Oprichnik: opera in four acts (Lazhechnikov/Tchaikovsky)
(1870–2)

Two Pieces for piano, Op. 10: *Nocturne*; *Humoresque* (1872)

Cantata for the bicentenary of Peter the Great (Polonsky) (1872)

'Vous l'ordonnez': couplets for Beaumarchais' *Le Barbier de Seville* (trans. Sadowsky) (1872)

Six Romances, Op. 16 (1872) :
'Lullaby' (Maikov);
'Wait' (Grekov);
'Accept just once' (Fet);
'O sing that song' (Hemans/Plescheyev);
'Thy radiant image' (Tchaikovsky);
'New Greek Song' (Maikov)

Symphony No. 2 in C minor, Op. 17
Little Russian (1872, revised with substantially altered first movement
1879–80)

Serenade for Nikolai Rubinstein's name-day (1872)

Incidental music to Ostrovsky's *The Snow Maiden* (1873)

The Tempest: symphonic fantasia, Op. 18 (1873)

'Take my heart away' (Fet) (1873)

'Blue eyes of spring' (Heine/Mikhailov) (1873)

Six Pieces for piano, Op. 19 (1873)

Six Pieces on a Single Theme for piano, Op. 21 (1873)

String Quartet No. 2 in F, Op. 22 (1874)

Vakula Kuznets (*Vakula the Smith* or *Les caprices d'Oxane*):
opera in four acts, Op. 14 (Gogol/Polonsky)
(1873; revised and renamed *Cherevichki* or *The Slippers* in 1885)

Piano Concerto No. 1 in B♭ minor, Op. 23 (1874–5)

Six Romances, Op. 25 (1874–5) :
'Reconciliation' (Shcherbina);
'As o'er the burning ashes' (Tyutchev);
'Mignon's Song' (Goethe/Tyutchev);
'The Canary' (Mey);
'I never spoke to her' (Mey);
'As they kept on saying, "fool"' (Mey)

Sérénade mélancolique for violin and orchestra, Op. 26 (1875)

Six Romances, Op. 27 (1875) :

'To sleep' (Ogarev);

'Look, yonder cloud' (Grekov);

'Do not leave me' (Fet);

'Evening' (Shevchenko/Mey);

'Was it the mother who bore me?' (Mickiewicz/Mey);

'My spoiled darling' (Mickiewicz/Mey)

Six Romances, Op. 28 (1875) :

'No, I shall never tell' (de Musset/Grekov);

'The Corals' (Syrokomla/Mey);

'Why did I dream of you' (Mey);

'He loved me so much' (anon);

'No response or word of greeting' (Apukhtin);

'The fearful minute' (Tchaikovsky)

'We have not far to walk': song (Grekov; 1875)

'I should like in a single word': song (Heine/Mey; 1875)

Cantata for the golden jubilee of Osip Petrov (Nekrasov) (1875)

Symphony No. 3 in D minor, Op. 29, *Polish* (1875)

Swan Lake: ballet in four acts, Op. 20 (1875–6)

The Seasons for piano, Op. 37b (1875–6)

String Quartet No. 3 in E♭ minor, Op. 30 (1876)

Marche slave (*Slavonic March*, originally entitled *Serbo-Russian March*), Op. 31 (1876)

Francesca da Rimini: symphonic fantasia, Op. 32 (1876)

Variations on a Rococo Theme, for cello and orchestra, Op. 33 (1876)

Symphony No. 4 in F minor, Op. 36 (1877)

Eugene Onegin: lyric scenes in three acts
(Pushkin/Shilovsky/Tchaikovsky), Op. 24 (1877–8)

Valse-scherzo for violin and orchestra, Op. 34 (1877)

Violin Concerto in D, Op. 35 (1878)

Piano Sonata in G, Op. 37 (1878)

Six Romances, Op. 38 (1878) :

'Don Juan's Serenade';

'It was in the early spring';

'Amid the din of the ball';

'O, if only you could for one moment' (all A. Tolstoy);

'The love of a dead man' (Lermontov);

'Pimpinella' (Tchaikovsky, after a traditional Florentine song)

Album for children: 24 easy pieces (à la Schumann) for piano, Op. 39 (1878)

Twelve Pieces of moderate difficulty for piano, Op. 40 (1878)

Liturgy of St. John Chrysostom, for unaccompanied chorus, Op. 41 (1878)

March for the Volunteer Fleet (Skobelev March)

Souvenir d'un lieu cher for violin and piano, Op. 42 (1878)

The Maid of Orléans: opera in four acts (Schiller/Zhukovsky/Tchaikovsky) (1878–9)

Suite No. 1 in D minor, Op. 43 (1878–9)

Piano Concerto No. 2 in G major, Op. 44 (1879–80; revised by Siloti with Tchaikovsky's approval, 1893)

Capriccio Italien, Op. 45 (1880)

Six Duets, Op. 46 (1880) :

'Evening' (Surikov);

'Edward' (Scottish ballad trans. A. Tolstoy);

'Tears' (Tryutchev);

'In the garden near the ford' (Shevchenko/Surikov);

'Passion spent' (A. Tolstoy);

'Dawn' (Surikov; also orch. Tchaikovsky)

Serenade in C major for string orchestra, Op. 48 (1880)

1812: festival overture, Op. 49 (1880)

Duet from Shakespeare's *Romeo and Juliet* (trans. Sokolovsky)
(1881 – possibly 1893 – completed by Taneyev)

Piano Trio in A minor, Op. 50 (1881–2)

Six Pieces for piano, Op. 51 (1882)

All-night Vigil, for unaccompanied chorus, Op. 52 (1881–2)

Mazeppa: opera in three acts (Pushkin/Burenin/Tchaikovsky) (1881–3)

Couplets on Glinka's *A Life for the Tsar*,
with the Russian National Anthem (1883)

Coronation March (1883)

Moscow: coronation cantata (Maikov) (1883)

Suite No. 2 in C major, Op. 53 (1883)

Sixteen Songs for Children, Op. 54 (1881–3) :

'Granny and Grandson';

'Little bird';

'Spring';

'My little garden';

'Legend: the Christ-child had a garden' (also orch. Tchaikovsky, 1884, and arranged for unaccompanied chorus, 1889);

'On the bank';

'Winter evening';

'The Cuckoo';

'The snow's already melting';

'Lullaby in a storm';

'The flower';

'Winter';

'Spring song';

'Autumn' (all Pleshcheyev);

'The swallow' (Lenartowicz/Surikov);

'Child's song' (Aksakov)

Concert Fantasia in G major for piano and orchestra, Op. 56 (1884)

Suite No. 3 in G major, Op. 55 (1884)

Impromptu caprice for piano (1884)

Elegy in honour of Ivan Samarin, for string orchestra
(1884, used in the incidental music to *Hamlet*, 1891)

Six Romances, Op. 57 (1884) :
'Tell me, what in the shade of the branches' (Sollogub);
'On the golden cornfields' (A. Tolstoy);
'Heiss mich nicht reden' (Goethe/Strugovshchikov);
'Sleep' ;
'Death' (both Merezhkovsky);
'Only thou' (Kristen/Pleshcheyev)

Nine Sacred Pieces for unaccompanied chorus (1884–5)

Manfred Symphony, Op. 58 (1885)

Hymn to St. Cyril and St. Methodius for unaccompanied chorus (1884–5)

Jurists' March; Jurists' Song for unaccompanied chorus (1885)

Cherevichki see under *Vakula the Smith*

Dumka for piano, Op. 59 (1886)

Twelve Romances, Op. 60 (1886) :
'Last night' (Khomyakov);
'I'll tell thee nothing' (Fet);
'O, if you knew' (Pleshcheyev);
'The nightingale' (Stefanovic/Pushkin);
'Simple words' (Tchaikovsky);
'Frenzied nights' (Apukhtin);
'Song of the gypsy girl' (Polonsky);
'Forgive!' (Nekrasov);
'Night';
'Behind the window, in the shadow';
'The mild stars shone for us' (all Polonsky);
'Exploit' (Khomyakov)

The Enchantress (*Charodeyka*): opera in four acts (Shpazhinsky) (1885–7)

Monologue for the Domovoy scene in Ostrovsky's *The Voyevoda* (1886)

Suite No. 4 in G *Mozartiana* (arrangements of Mozart: Gigue, K.574; Minuet, K.355; *Ave verum corpus*, K.618 – Liszt transcription; Variations on a theme by Gluck, K.455) (1887)

'An angel weeping' for unaccompanied chorus (1887)

'The golden cloud has slept' for unaccompanied chorus (Lermontov) (1887)

'Blessed is he who smiles' for unaccompanied male chorus (Grand Duke Konstantin) (1887)

Pezzo capriccioso for cello and orchestra, Op. 62 (1887)

Six Romances, Op. 63:

'I did not love you at first';

'I opened the window';

'I did not please you';

'The first tryst';

'The fires in the room were already extinguished';

'Serenade' (all Grand Duke Constantine; 1887)

Symphony No. 5 in E minor, Op. 64 (1888)

Six Romances on French texts, Op. 65 (1888) :

'Aurore' (Turquety);

'Deception';

'Serenade';

'Poeme d'octobre';

'Rondel' (all Collin);

'Les larmes' (Blanchecotte)

Hamlet: fantasy overture, Op. 67a (1888)

'The Nightingale' for unaccompanied chorus (Tchaikovsky) (1889)

The Sleeping Beauty ballet in a prologue and three acts, Op. 66 (1888–9)

Valse-scherzo for piano (1889)

Impromptu for piano (1889)

A Greeting to Anton Rubinstein,
for unaccompanied chorus (Polonsky) (1889)

The Queen of Spades (*Pikovaya Dama*): opera in three acts
(Pushkin/M. and P. Tchaikovsky), Op. 68 (1890)

The Voyevoda: symphonic ballad, Op. 78 (1890–1)

String Sextet in D major: *Souvenir de Florence*,
Op. 70 (1890; revised 1891)

Incidental music to Shakespeare's *Hamlet* (1891)

'Without time, without season' for unaccompanied women's chorus
(Tsiganov) (1891)

'The voice of mirth grew silent' for unaccompanied men's chorus
(Pushkin) (1891)

Yolanta: opera in one act (Herz/Zotov/M. Tchaikovsky),
Op.69 (1891)

The Nutcracker ballet in two acts, Op. 71 (1891; *Nutcracker* Suite,
Op. 71a 1892)

Aveu passione for piano (1892?)

Impromptu (*Momento lirico*) for piano
(1892–3, completed by Taneyev)

Symphony ('No. 7') in E♭ major
(1892, reconstructed by Bogatryev; first movement converted by
Tchaikovsky into Piano Concerto No. 3, 1893)

Eighteen Pieces for piano, Op. 72 (1893)

Piano Concerto No. 3 in E♭ major (one movement), Op. 75 (1893)

Military March for piano (short score for military band piece, 1893)

Six Romances, Op. 73:
'We sat together';
'Night';
'In the moonlight';
'The sun has set';
'Mid sombre days';
'Again, as before, alone' (all Rathaus; 1893)

Symphony No. 6 in B minor, Op. 74 *Pathétique* (1893)

The following list of recordings is included as a guide to some of the interpretations of Tchaikovsky's work available at the time of writing and is by no means intended as an exhaustive catalog. The works are listed first, followed by details of the recording, the artists, record company and disc number. All numbers given are those that apply to the compact disc format, but many recordings can also be bought on conventional tape cassette.

ORCHESTRAL

The Six Symphonies

LSO/Markevitch. Philips 426 848-2 (4 CDs)

Philharmonia/Muti (c/w *Romeo and Juliet*). EMI CZS 7671342 (4 CDs)

Symphonies 4–6

Leningrad PO/Mravinsky. DG 419 745-2 (2 CDs)

St. Petersburg PO/Temirkanov. RCA 09026 613772 (2 CDs)

Symphony No. 1, *Winter Daydreams* Opus 13
Chicago SO/Abbado (c/w *Nutcracker Suite*). Sony CD 48056

Symphony No.2, *Little Russian* – original version Opus 17
LSO/Simon. Chandos CHAN 8304

Symphony No.2, *Little Russian* – revised version Opus 17
Berlin PO/Karajan (c/w *1812* Overture)
DG 419 177-2

Symphony No.3, *Polish* Opus 29
Bournemouth SO/Litton
(c/w *Capriccio Italien*, Polonaise from *Eugene Onegin*)
Virgin VC 7 90761-2

Opus 36   Symphony No. 4

Vienna PO/Abbado (c/w Symphony No.2)

DG 431 604-2GR

Opus 64   Symphony No. 5

Philadelphia/Muti (c/w *Francesca da Rimini*)

EMI CDC 7 54338-2

Opus 74   Symphony No. 6, *Pathétique*

Russian National Orch/Pletnev (c/w *Marche slave*)

Virgin VC 7 91487 2

Czech PO/Matacíć (c/w *Capriccio Italien*).

Supraphon 2SUP0008

Manfred Symphony   Opus 58
NBC Symphony Orch/Toscanini
(recorded in 1949 – with cuts – c/w *Romeo and Juliet*).
RCA GD60298

The Storm   Opus 76
LSO/Rozhdestvensky (c/w *Pathétique* Symphony).
Pickwick PCDS 10

Fatum   Opus 77
The Voyevoda   Opus 78
St Louis SO/Slatkin (c/w Symphony No. 4).
RCA RD 60432

Romeo and Juliet
NBC Symphony Orch/Toscanini
(see under *Manfred*)

Opus 18   *The Tempest*
Chicago SO/Abbado
(c/w *Marche slave*; *1812* Overture; *Romeo and Juliet*).
Sony CD47179

Opus 31   *Marche slave*
Opus 49   *1812* Overture
Gothenburg SO/Järvi
(c/w orchestral works by Rimsky-Korsakov and Borodin).
DG 429 984-2

Francesca da Rimini Opus 32

Hamlet Opus 67a

New York Stadium SO/Stokowski.
Dell'Arte CDA9006

Capriccio Italien Opus 45

Oslo PO/Jansons (c/w Symphony No. 2).
Chandos CHAN8640

Serenade for strings Opus 48

USSR Ministry of Culture SO/Rozhdestvensky
(c/w *Francesca da Rimini*; *Marche slave*).
Erato 2292-45629 2

Suites 1–4

Much the best recording of the four suites,

Dorati's with the New Philharmonia on Philips,

has been unavailable for some time.

The following are interim recommendations for separate issues:

Opus 43   Suite No.1

USSR State Academy Orch/Svetlanov (c/w Suite No. 4).

Olympia OCD109

Opus 53   Suite No.2

Opus 61   Suite No. 4, *Mozartiana*

Philharmonia/Tilson Thomas.

CBS 46503

Opus 55   Suite No. 3

Festival Coronation March

USSR Ministry of Culture SO/Rozhdestvensky.

Erato 2292-45970-2

SOLO INSTRUMENT AND ORCHESTRA

Piano Concerto No. 1   Opus 23
Horowitz/NBC Symphony Orch/Toscanini
(recorded in 1941 – c/w piano works by Mussorgsky).
RCA GD60449
Richter/Vienna SO/Karajan
(c/w Rachmaninov Preludes).
DG 419 068-2GA

Piano Concerto No. 2 – original version   Opus 44
Piano Concerto No. 3
Donohoe/Bournemouth SO/Barshai.
EMI CDC7 49940-2

Opus 56   Concert Fantasia for piano and orchestra
Pletnev/Philharmonia/Fedoseyev
(c/w Piano Concerto No. 1).
Virgin VC7 91190-2

Opus 33   *Variations on a Rococo Theme* for cello and orchestra – original version
Opus 62   *Pezzo capriccioso*
Isserlis/COE/Gardiner
(c/w pieces by Glazunov, Rimsky-Korsakov and Cui).
Virgin VC7 91134-2

Violin Concerto　　Opus 35

Bell/Cleveland Orch/Ashkenazy

(c/w Wieniawski: Violin Concerto No. 2).

Decca 421 716-2

Valse-scherzo for violin and orchestra　　Opus 34

Perlman/Leningrad PO/Temirkanov

(part of the Tchaikovsky Gala in Leningrad).

RCA RD60739

CHAMBER MUSIC

String Quartets 1–3

Opus 70   *Souvenir de Florence* for string sextet

Borodin String Quartet/Bashmet/Gutman.

EMI CDS7 49775-2 (2 CDs)

Opus 50   Piano Trio

Heifetz/Piatigorsky/Rubinstein

(recorded in 1950 – c/w Mendelssohn: Piano Trio No. 1).

RCA GD87768

PIANO WORKS, SONGS AND CHORAL WORKS

Complete Piano Works

Postnikova.

Erato 2292-45969-2 (7 CDs)

The Seasons

Six Morceaux Composés Sur un Seul Thème   Opus 21

Pletnev.

Virgin VCS 45042-2

Songs

Söderström/Ashkenazy.

Decca 436 204-2DM

Songs

Vishnevskaya/Rostropovich

(c/w songs by Glinka, Borodin, Dargomyzhsky and Mussorgsky).

Erato 2292-45643-2 (2 CDs)

Songs

Borodina/Gegieva.

Philips 442 013-2

Songs

'A tear trembles';

'None but the lonely heart';

'Reconciliation';

'The fearful minute';

'Don Juan's serenade';

'The nightingale';

'Exploit';

'I opened the window';

'Again, as before, alone'

Hvorostovsky/Boshniakovich (c/w songs by Rachmaninov).

Philips 432 119-2PH

Opus 41   Liturgy of St John Chrysostom

Sacred Pieces

An Angel Crying

Leningrad Glinka Academy Ch/Chernushenko.

Le Chant du Monde LDC278 728

Opus 52   *All-night Vigil*

Sacred Pieces

Leningrad Glinka Academy Ch/Chernushenko.

Le Chant du Monde LDC278 749

Stage Works: Complete

The Snow Maiden – complete incidental music
Mishura-Lekhtman/Grishko/Detroit Symphony Orch and Ch/Järvì.
CHAN 9324

Swan Lake   Opus 20
Montreal Symphony Orch/Dutoit.
Decca 43b 212-2DH2 (2 CDs)

Opus 24   *Eugene Onegin*

Vishnevskaya/Belov/Lemeshev/Petrov/Bolshoi Theatre Ch and Orch/Khaikin (recorded in 1956).

BMG/Melodiya 74321170902 (2 CDs)

Mazeppa

Leiferkus/Gorchakova/Kotcherga/Diadkova/Carin/Gothenburg Symphony Orch/Järvi.

DG 439 906-2 (3 CDs)

The Sleeping Beauty   Opus 66

Royal Opera House Orch, Covent Garden/Ermler.

Conifer/Royal Opera House ROH306/8 (3 CDs)

The Queen of Spades   Opus 68

Grigorian/Guleghina/Putilin/Chernov/Arkhipova/Borodina/Kirov

Ch and Orch/Gergiev.

Philips 438 141-2 (3 CDs)

Opus 67a   *Hamlet* – incidental music

LSO/Simon

(c/w *Romeo and Juliet* – original version;

Serenade for Rubinstein;

Festival Overture;

Mazeppa – excerpts).

Chandos CHAN8310/1 (2 CDs)

Opus 69   *Yolanta*

Vishnevskaya/Gedda/Groenroos/Petkov/

Orch de Paris/Rostropovich.

Erato 2292-45973-2 (2 CDs)

The Nutcracker   Opus 71
LSO/Previn.
Classics for Pleasure CFPD 4706 (2 CDs)

STAGE WORKS: EXCERPTS

Eugene Onegin – Tatyana's Letter Scene   Opus 24
Beňacková/Czech PO/Neumann
(c/w Czech and Russian arias).
Supraphon 10 2843-2

The Maid of Orléans – Joan's aria

Norman/Leningrad PO/Temirkanov

(part of the Tchaikovsky Gala in Leningrad).

RCA RD60739

Baritone arias from *Eugene Onegin*, *Mazeppa*,

The Enchantress, *The Queen of Spades*, *Iolanta*.

Hvorostovsky/Rotterdam PO/Gergiev (c/w Verdi arias).

Philips 426 740-2PH

Opus 20   *Swan Lake* – highlights

Menuhin, Philharmonia/Kurtz.

Classics for Pleasure CD-CFP4926

Swan Lake, *The Sleeping Beauty*, *The Nutcracker* – highlights
LSO/Previn.
EMI Rouge et Noir CZS7 62816 2 (2 CDs) or EMI CDM7 64332 2

Swan Lake, *The Sleeping Beauty*, *The Nutcracker* – suites
Berlin PO/Rostropovich.
DG Galleria 429 097-2

The Nutcracker – Act Two   Opus 71
Scottish National Orch/Järvi (c/w *Swan Lake* selection).
Chandos CHAN 8556

AAM *Academy of Ancient Music*
arr. *arranged/arrangement*
ASMF *Academy of St. Martin-in-the-Fields*
attrib. *attributed*
bar. *baritone*
bc. *basso continuo*
bn. *bassoon*
c. *circa*
ch. *chorus/choir/chorale*
Chan. *Chandos*
cl. *clarinet*
CO *Chamber Orchestra*
COE *Chamber Orchestra of Europe*
comp. *composed/composition*
contr. *contralto*
db. *double bass*
DG *Deustche Grammophon*
Dig. *digital recording*
dir. *director*
ECO *English Chamber Orchestra*
ed. *editor/edited*
edn. *edition*
ens. *ensemble*
fl. *flute*
HM *Harmonia Mundi France*
hn. *horn*
hp. *harp*
hpd *harpsichord*
Hung. *Hungaroton*

instr. *instrument/instrumental*
kbd. *keyboard*
LSO *London Symphony Orchestra*
Mer. *Meridian*
mez. *mezzo-soprano*
ob. *oboe*
OCO *Orpheus Chamber Orchestra*
orch. *orchestra/orchestral/orchestrated*
org. *organ/organist*
O-L *Oiseau-Lyre*
perc. *percussion*
pf. *pianoforte*
picc. *piccolo*
PO *Philharmonic Orchestra*
qnt. *quintet*
qt. *quartet*
sop. *soprano*
str. *string(s)*
tb. *trombone*
ten. *tenor*
tpt. *trumpet*
trans. *translated/translation*
transcr. *transcribed/transcription*
unacc. *unaccompanied*
va. *viola*
var. *various/variation*
vc. *cello*
vn. *violin*

- SELECTED FURTHER READING -

David Brown, *Tchaikovsky* (four volumes hardback, two volumes paperback, Gollancz, 1978–1986)

Catherine Drinker Bowen and Barbara von Meck, *Beloved Friend:*
The Story of Tchaikovsky and Nadezhda von Meck (Hutchinson, 1937)

Edward Garden and Nigel Gotteri, ed., *To My Best Friend:*
Correspondence between Tchaikovsky and Nadezhda von Meck 1876-1878 (Oxford, 1993)

Nicholas John, ed., *Eugene Onegin* – ENO/Royal Opera Guide (John Calder/Riverrun Press, 1988)

Alexandra Orlova, ed., *Tchaikovsky: A Self-Portrait* (Oxford, 1990)

Nikolai Andreyevich Rimsky-Korsakov, *My Musical Life* (Faber, 1989)

Leonid Sidelnikov and Pribegina, Galina, *25 Days in America* (Moscow 'Muzyka', 1991)

Vladimir Stasov, *Selected Essays or Music* (Barnie and Rocklist, 1968)

John Warrack, *Tchaikovsky* (Hamish Hamilton, 1973)

Translations of Pushkin's *Eugene Onegin* (by Charles Johnston) and
The Queen of Spades (by Rosemary Edmonds) are available in Penguin

- ACKNOWLEDGEMENTS -

The publishers wish to thank the following copyright holders for their permission to reproduce
illustrations supplied:

Archiv Für Kunst und Geschichte, London
The Bridgeman Art Library
Catherine Ashmore, Zoë Dominic
Private Collection, Lebrecht Collection
Lebrecht Collection
The Mansell Collection Ltd

1. ROMEO AND JULIET OVERTURE 20'39"
Boston Symphony Orchestra/Sir Colin Davis
*Tchaikovsky's first orchestral masterpiece, a perfect balance between the Russian
orthodox solemnity of the opening (a portrait of Shakespeare's Friar Laurence), the tense
rhythms of the fight sequences and the lyricism of the famous love music – tinged with a
note of autobiographical poignancy.*

2. 'NONE BUT THE LONELY HEART' 3'03"
Dmitri Hvorostovsky, baritone; Oleg Boshniakovich, piano
*The most famous of all Tchaikovsky's songs, and one of the earliest. It comes from the
Op.6 set and is a tender, nostalgic treatment of Mignon's second song of longing from
Goethe's Wilhelm Meister – also set, in the original German, by Beethoven,
Schubert, Schumann and Wolf.*

3. PIANO CONCERTO NO. 1, FINALE 6'30"
Werner Haas, Orchestre National de l'Opera de Monte-Carlo/Eliahu Inbal
*A surprisingly light and racy finale to an ambitious and large scale concerto,
contrasting the lively adaptation of a Ukrainian folksong with one of Tchaikovsky's
most attractive lyrical themes.*

4. SWAN LAKE, PAS DE DEUX 5'18"

Hugh Maguire, violin; London Symphony Orchestra/Pierre Monteux

Not the famous lakeside reverie for the Prince and Swan Queen, but an equally distinguished number for revellers at the First Act birthday celebrations often transferred to Act Three as a Pas de Deux for Siegfried and the treacherous decoy Odile. A dashing waltz – one of many in the ballet – leads to the heart of the dance, with a capricious and difficult solo for violin.

5. EUGENE ONEGIN, TATYANA'S LETTER SCENE 13'17"

Nuccia Focile, Orchestre de Paris/Semyon Bechov

The first part of the opera to be composed, this crucial scene in which the seventeen-year-old Tatyana impulsively writes a letter to the fascinating but aloof Onegin is a perfect mirror of youthful love's hopes and fears. Tchaikovsky clearly identified with his heroine's tender emotions.

6. SERENADE FOR STRINGS, WALTZ 3'47"

London Symphony Orchestra/Leopold Stokowski

Another waltz of great charm and ingenuity; the melody is typical of Tchaikovsky's ingenious way with a simple rising scale.

7. THE SLEEPING BEAUTY, ROSE ADAGIO 6'41"
Kirov Orchestra, St Petersburg/Valery Gergiev
A fulsomely romantic Pas d'action for Princess Aurora's birthday-party dance with four princely suitors, each of which in turn presents her with a rose.

8. THE NUTCRACKER, DANCE OF THE SUGAR PLUM FAIRY 2'10"
9. THE NUTCRACKER, DANCE OF THE REED PIPES 2'32"
Royal Concertgebouw Orchestra/Antal Dorati
The Sugar Plum Fairy's variation in the grand Pas de Deux *is Tchaikovsky's second, and most celebrated, employment of the (then) newly-discovered celesta mustel, elegantly accompanied at first by pizzicato strings and bass clarinet. The* Dance of the Reed Pipes *is another specimen of piquant scoring: this time the three orchestral flutes, and at one point the two trumpets, are in the spotlight.*

10. SYMPHONY NO. 6 'PATHÉTIQUE', FINALE 9'45"
London Symphony Orchestra/Igor Markevitch
The first significant slow-movement finale in the history of the symphony, a passionately protesting Adagio lamentoso. Tchaikovsky composed it in good health and high spirits, with no inkling of the untimely death in store; inevitably it came to be seen as his own requiem.